D0072784

DATE DUE

OCT 0 4 2007	
11-6-07	
GAYLORD	PRINTED IN U.S.A.

THE **XYZ** AFFAIR

Recent titles in
Contributions in American History

Series Editor: Jon L. Wakelyn

THE **XYZ** AFFAIR

William Stinchcombe

CONTRIBUTIONS IN AMERICAN HISTORY, NUMBER 89

GREENWOOD PRESS
WESTPORT, CONNECTICUT • LONDON, ENGLAND

Grateful acknowledgement is made to the following for permission to reprint:

Journal of American History for "Talleyrand and the American Negotiations of 1797-1798" by William Stinchcombe, 62 (December 1975): 575-90.

American Philosophical Society, for "A Neglected Memoir by Talleyrand on French-American Relations" by William Stinchcombe, *Proceedings* 121 (1977): 195-208.

William and Mary Quarterly for "The Diplomacy of the WXYZ Affair" by William Stinchcombe, 34 (1977): 590-617.

The Adams Manuscript Trust, Massachusetts Historical Society, for quotations from the Adams Papers.

Library of Congress Cataloging in Publication Data

Stinchcombe, William C
    The XYZ affair.

    Contributions in American history ; no. 89
ISSN 0084-9219)
        Bibliography: p.
        Includes index.
        1. United States—Foreign relations—France.
2. France—Foreign relations—United States.
3. United States—History—War with France, 1798-1800.
4. United States—Foreign relations—1797-1801.
5. France—Foreign relations—1792-1815. I. Title.
E323.S86   327.73044   80-544
ISBN 0-313-22234-7 (lib. bdg.)

Library of Congress Catalog Card Number: 80-544
ISBN: 0-313-22234-7
ISSN: 0084-9219

First published in 1980

Greenwood Press
A division of Congressional Information Service, Inc.
88 Post Road West, Westport, Connecticut 06881

Printed in the United States of America

10 9 8 7 6 5 4 3 2 1

To Jean

Contents

Illustrations

Preface

This work began when Stephen G. Kurtz asked me to work with him on the papers of John Marshall on the subject of Marshall's mission to Paris. Later Thad Tate and Charles T. Cullen encouraged me to undertake a separate treatment of the XYZ affair. I also incurred debts to Bradford Perkins, who offered appraisals drawn from his knowledge of the era. Among the scholars who shared information and documents with me, I particularly wish to thank George Billias, Lee Kennett, Brian Morton, and Romauld Szramkiewicz. My colleagues J. Roger Sharp and Stephen S. Webb read chapters of the manuscript and offered useful advice. Jon Wakelyn expressed enthusiasm about the project long before he became editor of this book. I thank them all.

Financial support for my research was provided by the Appleby Fund of the Maxwell School of Syracuse University and the Penrose Fund of the American Philosophical Society. Parts of the book have appeared in different form in the American Philosophical Society *Proceedings*, the *Journal of American History*, and the *William and Mary Quarterly* and are used with permission. The Adams Family Papers are quoted with the permission of the Massachusetts Historical Society.

My wife Jean's ability as a critic and an editor has made this a much better book than it would have been otherwise. Suffice it to say that the work would not have been done without her.

William Stinchcombe

THE **XYZ** AFFAIR

1

"Their Names Shall In No Event be Made Public"

Charles C. Pinckney, Elbridge Gerry, and John Marshall, the special envoys to France, already had spent almost three weeks in Paris before they first met in October 1797 with Jean Hottinguer and Pierre Bellamy, Talleyrand's agents, to discuss peace terms between the United States and France. The French agents proposed that the United States assume the vast private American claims against the French government, finance a loan in Dutch notes at double the market rate, offer an apology for President John Adams's speech of 16 May 1797, and provide a bribe of 50,000 pounds for Talleyrand's use. The envoys quickly explained the results of their first series of meetings with the French representatives in a dispatch to Secretary of State Timothy Pickering. In conclusion, they added that "the nature of the above communication will evince the necessity of secrecy," noting that they had assured Hottinguer and Bellamy "that their names shall in no event be made public." [1]

Although the envoys prepared their dispatch in the last week of October, delivery to the government in Philadelphia depended on a trustworthy merchant sailing to the United States. Because few ships departed from France and the Netherlands in the winter season, a long delay ensued. Anxious members of the Adams administration heard nothing from the envoys until 4 March 1798, when three dispatches arrived. Within the next three days two more arrived, presenting Pickering and Adams with a detailed account of the negotiations to mid-January. Adams announced to Congress that he saw no possibility of success for the special mission to France. But Republicans in Congress remained unconvinced and demanded the actual dispatches. Also inspired by the Federalists and members of the administration, Congress insisted that the president release the envoys' dispatches.

Two weeks before presenting the documents to Congress on 3 April 1798 Pickering had advised the envoys that the Senate and House of Representatives would probably call for the record of their negotiations and the president "will probably be under the necessity of doing it only withholding the two names which you promised should in no event be made public."[2] Pickering gleefully submitted the dispatches, substituting the letters, W, X, Y, and Z for Nicholas Hubbard, Jean Hottinguer, Pierre Bellamy, and Lucien Hauteval. The Senate and House ordered copies of the dispatches to be printed for the American public to read. Newspapers throughout the United States carried the entire account of the distasteful negotiations. Because W received only one or two mentions in the printed version of the dispatches, the negotiations soon became known in American history as the XYZ affair. Months after the publication of the dispatches, even John Marshall and Elbridge Gerry used the initials, not the names, of the French agents in discussing the merits of actions in Paris in the previous fall.[3]

The XYZ affair has drawn the interest of historians since 1798, in part because of its counterpoint of venality and virtue. American diplomats had withstood the blandishments and intimidation of the amoral Talleyrand and the corrupt diplomacy he practiced. Drama aside, the XYZ affair offered a complete account of intricate diplomatic negotiations, a record not surpassed in the United States' first seventy years as a nation. In the 1830s Congress ordered the publication of documents pertaining to the foundation of American foreign policy. The series of papers, entitled the *American State Papers*, included all of the previously published XYZ documents, thus allowing generations of scholars and students access to the story. Many nineteenth-century Americans drew a simple moral from the XYZ affair: it revealed the fundamental, continuing corruption of Europe.

For historians, too, the context and implications of the XYZ affair—really the WXYZ affair—continued to hold interest long into the twentieth century. The French Revolution, more than the American, was the preeminent political event of the period, influencing European statesmen and politics well into the nineteenth century. The French Revolution, beginning in 1789, stimulated a period of intense public debate about the purpose of American foreign policy. From President Washington's proclamation of neutrality in 1793 until the Convention of Mortefontaine with France in 1801, which officially ended the French-American alliance of 1778, the very definition of the United States as a nation and Americans as a people was being debated. In this distinctive era Americans saw each other not so much as Federalists or Republicans or Yankees or Southerners but as Jacobins or Monocrats.

The period of the 1790s witnessed sudden shifts in opinion during a protracted, bitter controversy over the proper American policy toward France. The crisis in French-American relations dated back to 1793, at the outbreak of war between France and Great Britain. At that time Washington had asked members of his cabinet to submit their opinions on what policy the United States should pursue. In the lengthy cabinet debate that followed, Hamilton contended that the French alliance was no longer in effect because it had been signed with a monarchy. Washington quickly rejected Hamilton's interpretation and announced that the United States would honor its commitments under the alliance. Washington's reaction was partly influenced by Jefferson's argument that France would never require the United States to fulfill its obligations. Jefferson reasoned that the French understood that the United States could not and would not honor these obligations. But he thought that the United States should publicly uphold the alliance because it guaranteed American independence. Jefferson expressed relief when Edmond Charles Edouard Genet, the French minister to the United States, informed him that France would not call upon the United States to guarantee its West Indian colonies.[4] Washington's proclamation of neutrality in 1793 was a formal statement that the United States would shape its foreign policy with the objective of staying out of the newest French-British war.

The public accepted Washington's pronouncement with little dissent, and Congress passed enabling legislation (mainly shipping and seamen's laws) to implement it. This was to be Washington's last major act in foreign policy that did not provoke bitter controversy in the United States. A few critics accused the president of turning his back on republican France, but only the bitterly anti-British Jeffersonian poet and journalist Philip Freneau pointed out that neutrality was contrary to the French alliance.[5]

Washington believed that his policy of strict neutrality in combination with outspoken approval of the French Revolution would enable the United States to maintain friendly relations with France. Until 1797, his last year in office, Washington remained more optimistic than most Federalists, including John Adams, about the eventual success of the French Revolution.[6]

Relations with France already had become sensitive by 1792, however, when Washington appointed Gouverneur Morris to succeed Jefferson as minister to France. Senate debate over Morris's appointment revealed the politically charged character of the position. George Mason believed that to appoint Morris with "his known monarchical principles had rather the appearance of Insult, than of Compliment or Congratulation." Morris would not have been "displeasing at the Court of Petersburg or Berlin; but is surely very ill suited to that of Paris."[7] Morris as United States minister in Paris made no effort to hide his sympathies and worked overtly with the Royalists. Outspoken in his opinions, Morris told David Humphries, "I was desired in a large Society to draw the Horoscope of France to which I answered that it might be done in three words *Guerre Famine Peste.*"[8]

Despite his personal feelings, Morris believed that although many Americans had been injured by French policy, "yet the Government means well towards us."[9] Local violations, such as forbidding American ships to embark, failing to make payment under contracts made with Americans, and imprisoning American citizens, resulted more from the chaos of revolution than from a conscious national policy, Morris believed. He attempted to defend American interests without provoking the French government and emphasized the precariousness of French policy in the revolution's rapid changes. When Washington had Genet recalled for his many transgressions, Jefferson urged that Morris, too, be recalled because he was unacceptable to the French government, and the president did so. Although hurt that he was recalled because of "faction," Morris himself had once said, "if I get thro this mission honorably it will be a Master Piece, and yet nine out of ten will say it was the easiest Thing in Nature."[10]

Washington then asked Robert R Livingston to succeed Morris, but Livingston pleaded other commitments. James Monroe, also under consideration for the post, heard of Livingston's refusal and asked his colleague from revolutionary days why he had rebuffed Washington. He informed Monroe that he could not accept the position because he was out of sympathy with the policies of the Washington administration.[11] Washington next asked Monroe, who accepted the position with alacrity. In 1793, then, Washington's first two choices were men well disposed toward France and in Monroe's case even enthusiastic about the French Revolution.

As minister to France, Monroe filled the position in the same spirit as had Morris. He appeared before the National Convention to present his credentials, even though he knew that such a step would be misinterpreted in the United States as excessively sympathetic to France and the French Revolution. He explained to his political ally from Virginia, James Madison, that his action was necessary because the French had lost a great deal of confidence in the United States, which he sought to restore.[12] He considered France essentially friendly to the United States and took pains to negotiate for the release of Americans in French prisons and of confiscated ships on a case-by-case basis, making certain that he never accused France of belligerent intentions toward the United States.

Initially, Great Britain and France welcomed the American proclamation of neutrality as each country attempted to impel the United States to interpret neutrality in its favor. France originally held the advantage under the neutrality proclamation, because the French alliance of 1778 sanctioned French use of American ports to conduct privateering raids on Spanish and British shipping in the West Indies. Because the United States had exploited neutrality by carrying products from the West Indies to France and the Netherlands, in 1794 Great Britain restricted neutral shipping and captured and condemned hundreds of American vessels, thus bringing the two countries to the verge of war.

Congress then passed a temporary embargo on trade, and Washington at the same time sought to avoid war and economic reprisals by appointing John Jay as minister extraordinary to Great

Britain, superseding the resident minister, Thomas Pinckney. Jay's
instructions were to negotiate a commercial treaty and settle as
many of the outstanding differences between the two countries as
possible but not to sign any treaty that would conflict with the
French alliance. Edmund Randolph, the secretary of state, asked
that Monroe inform the French government of Jay's instructions
and emphasized to him "how indispensable it is that you should
keep the French Republic in good humor with us."[13]

Jay concluded a treaty with Great Britain that gave a number of
advantages to the United States. Foremost among these gains
would be ten years of commercial stability with the United States as
a favorite trading partner. Forts at Oswegatchie, Oswego, and
Niagara in New York protecting the St. Lawrence valley and the
entrance to Lake Erie were turned over to the Americans. Two
other forts at Detroit and Michimackinack in Michigan were also
given up, at last fulfilling the British promise made in the peace
treaty of 1783. Boundary commissions would finally settle disputes
arising from the 1783 peace treaty. Another commission would
determine how much Great Britain was liable for damages for
captured American shipping. Jay also agreed to a redefinition of
the meaning of neutral goods, reversing the policy of "free ships
make free goods" that had been the basis of the commercial treaty
with France in 1778.

Jay sent John Trumbull to Paris to explain the treaty to James
Monroe. Monroe asked for a copy of the treaty, but when Trumbull
asked for assurances that it would not be given to the French
government, Monroe refused. Although Monroe opposed Jay's
Treaty, he believed that if he had the contents he would have a year
to try to accommodate French objections to it. He continued to
believe, long after his recall, that France eventually would have
accepted the Jay Treaty.[14]

The treaty's arrival in the United States set off a prolonged
foreign policy debate even more vigorous than that provoked by
Genet's actions in 1793. After the Senate began discussion of the
treaty, its contents were leaked to a Republican newspaper. Widespread protests deplored the sacrifice of the American neutrality
policy to the interests of merchants and the might of the British
navy. The Senate ratified the treaty by a bare twenty-to-ten mar-

gin. Washington considered the treaty inadequate and delayed signing it.

The crucial turning point for Washington and for Federalist policy toward France came in the dismissal of Edmund Randolph as secretary of state in 1795. Randolph had held a number of indiscreet conversations with French minister Joseph Fauchet, who replaced Genet, openly inviting French participation in internal American politics. The British intercepted Fauchet's descriptions of the conversations and turned them over to the United States. After hearing Randolph's lame explanation, Washington rightly demanded his immediate resignation. On the same day, however, the president also signed Jay's Treaty, on the strong advice of his entire cabinet, including Randolph. The firing of Randolph and the signing of the Jay treaty became inseparably linked in the public mind. By then Washington's opposition so distrusted the president that Joel Barlow commented on Randolph's firing "that Robespierre never sacrificed a man on slighter grounds."[15]

When four men declined Washington's offer to become secretary of state, the president was compelled to choose his secretary of war, Timothy Pickering, an acidly anti-French Federalist from Massachusetts. Washington's increasing disillusionment with prominent Republicans now led him to choose advisers with known anti-French views, while he had earlier called upon men who viewed France as a permanent counterweight to Great Britain. Now this view of France, commonly associated with Jefferson and Madison but also advanced by Randolph, Monroe, and Robert Livingston, no longer had an effective advocate in cabinet deliberations.

Yet the debate over Jay's Treaty did not end with Washington's signing it. Led by Madison, the Republicans in the House of Representatives insisted that the money required to finance the various commissions authorized by the Jay Treaty gave the House a role in the treaty-making process. In a long and exceptionally bitter debate in the early months of 1796, the Republicans tried to defeat the treaty by denying funds. Pierre Adet, who succeeded Fauchet as French minister to the United States, expected the Republicans to succeed and advised his government to wait before reacting to the Jay Treaty. In July 1796, however, the House approved the necessary appropriations by three votes.

By the last months of his term, Washington felt that Monroe favored the French too much and, accepting Pickering's complaints, recalled his minister in disgrace. Washington's shift in attitude toward France was also apparent when he turned to John Marshall and then Charles C. Pinckney to succeed Monroe. Neither had a reputation for being pro-French, much less a reputation for being sympathetic to the French Revolution. Washington stipulated that the new minister to France must be one "who will not thwart the neutrality policy of the government and at the same time will not be obnoxious to the People among whom he is sent."[16] Neither Washington nor Adams in the following year realized that these points could not be reconciled in the appointment of Pickney and then Marshall—that the two goals were contradictory to many Frenchmen.[17]

By the fall of 1796 Washington had moved into the anti-French ranks of the high Federalists. Stung by an unfamiliar but growing opposition to his foreign policy, Washington delivered his Farewell Address. The address was rewritten largely by Hamilton, who had concluded that the French "alliance in its future operations must be against our Interest. A door to escape from it is opened."[18] In the context of debate over French policy the address can only be considered a partisan document defending the Federalists. In the Farewell Address he castigated the French and French influence in no uncertain terms.

Privately, Washington used even stronger language to condemn the French. He argued that the behavior of France toward the United States "is, according to my ideas of it, outrageous beyond conception; not to be warranted by her treaties with us; by the Law of Nations; by any principle of justice; or even by a regard to decent appearances."[19] Only a Federalist of exceedingly limited understanding such as Roger Griswold, a representative from Connecticut, could write in the last week of 1796 that "the French subject is at present quite still, & little danger need be apprehended of any serious controversy with that nation."[20]

In the first three years of the Adams administration came the XYZ affair, precipitating the Quasi-War, followed by the appointment of a second commission to France in 1799, and finally negotiation of an acceptable treaty with France in 1801. Any and all of these events have long interested historians, and the inextricable combination of domestic politics and diplomacy has been particularly intriguing.

The roles of Adams, Jefferson, Talleyrand, and Hamilton can be better understood by an examination of the WXYZ negotiations from October 1797 to April 1798. Many issues were resolved; other problems were found insuperable. Both nations remained close to war in the summer of 1798, but they were still closer to peace than they had been in 1797. No definitive accounting can be given of Adams's or Talleyrand's motives or actions, but broad trends and consistencies in their policies can be seen. That the XYZ affair had a profound effect on American partisan politics is undeniable. But that is not to say that President Adams and his conflicts with Hamiltonian Federalists or even the division between the Federalists and the Jeffersonian Republicans was primarily responsible for the affair. French officials believed that the United States had abrogated the French alliance, while American leaders remained equally convinced that the French had violated American rights.

The long, strained negotiations between the two nations helped to clear away any emotional attachments to republicanism and revolution that had influenced both Frenchmen and Americans. Leaving ideological commitments aside, differences between the two countries remained fundamental but manageable. Americans who believed that two republics should not fight each other, as did some Republicans, and others who sought to crush France as a revolutionary monster, as did some Federalists, shouted slogans, not policy. To achieve peace was a complicated, tenuous process, and in the end Talleyrand and Adams made the necessary decisions to secure it, realizing its ambiguity and frailty. To understand the conclusion, however, we must return to the negotiations that set these events in train.

Notes

1. American Envoys to Timothy Pickering, 22 October 1797, "Diplomatic Despatches, France," 6, Record Group 59, National Archives, Washington, D.C.

2. Timothy Pickering to American Envoys, 23 March 1798, "Diplomatic and Consular Instructions of the Department of State, 1791-1801," 1, Record Group 59, National Archives, Washington, D.C.

3. John Marshall to Elbridge Gerry, 12 November 1798, John Marshall Papers, College of William and Mary, Williamsburg, Virginia.

4. Dumas Malone, *Jefferson and the Ordeal of Liberty* (Boston, 1962), pp. 39-131; Jefferson to James Madison, 19 May 1793, James Madison Papers, Library of Congress, Washington, D.C.

5. Esther Brown, *The French Revolution and the American Man of Letters* (Columbia, Missouri, 1951), p. 113.

6. James Flexner, *George Washington: Anguish and Farewell*, 4 vols. (Boston, 1972), 4: 19, 257; Page Smith, *John Adams*, 2 vols. (New York, 1962), 2: 785-86, 882.

7. George Mason to James Monroe, 30 January 1792, James Monroe Papers, Library of Congress, Washington, D.C.

8. Gouverneur Morris to David Humphries, 5 June 1793, Gouverneur Morris Papers, Library of Congress, Washington, D.C.

9. Morris to Daniel Coxe, 22 March 1794, *ibid.*.

10. Morris to Robert Morris, 25 June 1793, *ibid.*.

11. Robert R Livingston to James Monroe, 16 May 1794, Monroe Papers.

12. Monroe to James Madison, 2 September 1794, Madison Papers.

13. Edmund Randolph to James Monroe, 25 September 1794, Monroe Papers.

14. Albert Gallatin to Hannah Gallatin, 28 June 1797, Albert Gallatin Papers, New-York Historical Society, New York, New York.

15. Joel Barlow to James Monroe, 18 October 1796, Monroe Papers.

16. George Washington to Timothy Pickering, 8 July 1796, Washington Papers, Library of Congress, Washington, D.C.

17. Max Fajn, "Le 'Journal des hommes libres des tous le pays' et les relations diplomatiques entre la France et les États-Unis de 1792 à 1800," *Revue D'Histoire Diplomatique* 85 (1971): 120-26.

18. Alexander Hamilton to Oliver Wolcott, Jr., 22 November 1796 in *The Papers of Alexander Hamilton*, 26 vol. ed. Harold Syrett et al. (New York, 1961-1979) 20: 414.

19. George Washington to Alexander Hamilton, 22 January 1797 in *ibid.*, p. 476.

20. Roger Griswold to Fanny Griswold, 28 December 1796, Griswold Family Papers, Yale University, New Haven, Connecticut.

2

"We Must Assume More Decorum"

In March 1797, John Adams and Thomas Jefferson, newly elected president and vice-president, arrived in Philadelphia for the swearing-in ceremonies. During the inaugural festivities, Adams asked Jefferson if he would accept a special appointment to France to negotiate the differences that had brought the two republics to the verge of war. Both men, however, developed second thoughts about the dignity of sending the vice-president to France, and Adams proposed instead that James Madison should be offered the position.[1]

Two days after the inauguration, the onetime political allies and friends departed together from a farewell party for Washington. Jefferson recalled that "as soon as we got onto the street I told him the event of my negociation with Mr. Madison," who refused the offer of appointment. Adams then revealed that "some objections to that nomination had been raised which he had not contemplated and going on with excuses which evidently embarrassed him." As the president and vice-president continued along the empty streets of Philadelphia, they examined the critical French issue, a problem that was to plague Adams throughout his term. Already a basic difference had developed between the two men on how to handle the problem with France. "When we came to 5th street where our road separated." Jefferson noted two months later, "we took leave and he never after that said one word to me on the subject or ever consulted me as to any measures."[2]

The widening breach between France and the United States would have created inevitable difficulties for any president. Once

an ally and treaty partner of the United States, the French government had reacted angrily to the approval of Jay's Treaty with Great
Britain. To the French, this treaty not only violated the alliance of
1778 but signaled in its place a virtual alliance between Great
Britain and the United States. Until July 1796, when the House of
Representatives voted the necessary funds to implement the treaty's
provisions, the French made few belligerent moves. In the fall of
1796, however, French reprisals came swiftly as French agents in
the West Indies, particularly Victor Hughes, authorized the capture
and sale of American ships and cargoes. In metropolitan France,
increased retaliation brought confiscation of American maritime
trade under the authority of several government decrees.

During the presidential campaign of 1796, the French minister to
the United States, Pierre Adet, had openly intervened on Jefferson's behalf. In speeches and a series of letters published in
Republican papers Adet charged that a Federalist victory would
make the United States a pawn of the British. In an effort to
influence the heavy Quaker vote in Pennsylvania, he predicted war
between the United States and France unless the Federalists were
turned out of office. After the election Adet notified the American
government that he had been recalled and that the French government would appoint no successor. Simultaneously, the French
government refused to receive Charles C. Pinckney of South Carolina as United States minister to France, although this was not yet
officially known in the United States.[3]

Among his contemporaries John Adams had the much-deserved
reputation of being an outspoken, persistent critic of the French
Revolution. But his policy in the opening months of his presidency
shows, on the contrary, a sustained effort to reach accommodation
with France—a change of tone and emphasis from the last days of
the Washington administration. The new president's policy, which
he made clear to neither Federalists nor Republicans, had two
interconnected components. He sought negotiations, not war, with
France over disputed issues; he stressed a commitment to neutrality and Jay's Treaty. Although the Jay Treaty aroused French distrust the most, Adams did not think American support for it offered
justification for France to go to war. The second part of Adams's
original policy was the appointment of negotiators friendly to
France, as his approaches to Jefferson and Madison demonstrated.

In the partisan atmosphere of the day, this policy would have required his forcing Federalists to accept the selection of a prominent Republican, as we shall discuss. A complete expression of Adams's peaceful intentions can be seen, however, in the final instructions written for the American envoys in July 1797, directives that stress accommodation as their goal. Reading the instructions for the first time in the summer of 1798, Jefferson admitted that they were moderate, not warlike.[4]

Yet Adams's policy had only limited success. He failed to persuade Republicans to serve under him, nor did the high Federalist wing of his own party approve of the selection of Republican envoys to France. The president's policy did not survive the country's deep partisan divisions, to which Adams himself had contributed. These partisan suspicions made Adams appear to be more hostile to France and to Republicans than he wished to be. The president's forced alliance with the high Federalists of his inherited cabinet, whose anti-French sentiments he never sufficiently repudiated, caused the Republicans to distrust him further. One French observer noted that Adams was a man between parties rather than above them as he liked to envision himself.[5]

During his eight years as vice-president, Adams had rarely spoken out on public issues, and consequently few people actually knew his view on French-American relations. Shortly after Adams's election, the French consul in Philadelphia, Joseph Létombe, called on the president. An acquaintance of Adams since the American Revolution, Létombe left the meeting pleased by Adams's pacific tone and surprised by his lack of belligerence toward France. Jefferson wrote to a skeptical Madison, who had distrusted and disliked Adams since the American Revolution, that he did "not believe Mr. A[dams] wishes war with France. Nor do I believe he will truckle to England as servilely as has been done." As he reviewed his mission, Adet found himself not optimistic but convinced nonetheless that Adams wanted peace with France. The element of surprise in these reactions highlights the widely accepted characterization of Adams as he took office; even informed observers knew few details of the policy Adams would pursue.[6]

Adams himself had contributed to widespread misunderstanding by his known distrust of the French Revolution. His policy toward France, however, did not stem from personal convictions about its revolution, which he felt certain would not permanently establish a republican form of government in France.[7] He objected to the profuse declarations of republican affinity between the United States and France made by some Americans, most notably the recently recalled United States minister to France, James Monroe. "We must assume more Decorum," he wrote in early 1797, "than to run after foreign Ministers as if We were their Slaves or Subjects." Adams considered the French Revolution an internal affair for Frenchmen, not a subject upon which Americans should comment, least of all Americans in official positions.[8] Beneath his strictures on dignity and decorum, however, lay a thinly disguised hostility not only to the French Revolution but to its partisans in the United States. But, this attitude did not determine foreign policy. Instead, Adams acted on the principle that interests—neutrality and Jay's Treaty—not ideology, should guide American diplomacy.

Adams saw a connection between Americans supporting the French Revolution and the French government's disregard for the United States. Echoing Washington's Farewell Address of the previous fall, the new president suggested that when Americans praised the French Revolution's republicanism, they offered an opportunity for French intervention in American domestic politics. Adams had long worried about French influence in the United States, a concern that had led to his break with the French foreign minister, Count de Vergennes, in Paris in 1781 as well as to his low opinion of Benjamin Franklin. If France would stop encouraging the Republicans, then the "French Party," as Adams labeled it when convenient, could be persuaded to treat France on the same basis as England. Adams linked upholding the Jay Treaty with national dignity, even sovereignty. According to his dubious reasoning, if the Republicans ceased their opposition to the Jay Treaty, the French would accept it, thus opening the way to a more stable peace for the United States. "The common saying here [in Philadelphia] is that it is an interposition of Providence that has saved me, defeated [Thomas] Pinckney, and disappointed the English party as well as the French," Adams wrote. He continued in a vein that would have astounded both Republicans and Federalists but represented the essence of his policy, "The French however are deceived, I am more their Friend than they are aware of."[9]

Adams's conception of himself as a man above parties made him appear, at best, equivocal on French policy. His offer to Jefferson created permanent suspicion among Federalists and Republicans. When old friends, which meant revolutionary Whigs to Adams, warned of political opposition to his policies, the president discounted their opinions. Elbridge Gerry and Elkanah Watson expressed their dismay at the mounting opposition of Alexander Hamilton and Timothy Pickering, secretary of state, but Adams ignored their advice. Holding an inflated image of himself as a leader, the president argued that he need not worry about this so-called opposition.[10]

The initial approaches to Jefferson and Madison demonstrated the difficulties of Adams's politics and perhaps his personality. Offering little or no consultation with members of his cabinet, the president sought to move quickly on a difficult issue. By appointing a known friend of France from the ranks of the opposition party, Adams hoped to find a solution to a pressing political and diplomatic problem. But to make his solution possible, he would have to make it politically acceptable.

Adams received some hint of future problems with his cabinet when he mentioned the possibility of Madison's appointment to Oliver Wolcott, Jr., secretary of the treasury. According to Adams's reconstruction of the conversation, which is indirectly supported by Jefferson, Wolcott threatened resignation if Madison were selected. Wolcott had not spoken in this manner to President Washington.[11] During Washington's tenure, Wolcott had accepted presidential decisions, but following the change of administrations, he decided to assert his prerogatives. Having been elected president by a small margin, Adams had started his term with a political position that was weak at best; from Federalists as well as Republicans he had limited support. He lacked the ability, personal as well as political, to persuade men to follow his leadership, a deficiency that he failed to detect in Madison's offhand dismissal of his proposal and Wolcott's partisan outburst.

In this instance, Adams could have found powerful support for Madison's appointment in an unexpected place, but he failed to exploit it. Alexander Hamilton, who had schemed against Adams in 1792 and 1796, just as he would do again in 1800, agreed with the president on the necessity of negotiating with France and appointing Madison as a special envoy to that country. Sensing Federalists' opposition to Madison as the sole envoy, Hamilton revised his opinion to call for appointing Madison as one of a three-man commission. To William L. Smith, Hamilton wrote, "I am clearly of the opinion for an extraordinary mission and as clearly that it should *embrace* Madison." He advanced this idea to at least three members of the cabinet—Wolcott, Pickering, and James McHenry, secretary of war. But with the exception of McHenry, Hamilton's pleadings went unheeded. Smith replied that "Madison has done so much to prostrate this Country at the feet of France, that I fear his appointmt. would appear humiliating & give disgust to our Friends." Surprisingly, Pickering suggested that instead of Madison or Jefferson, Joel Barlow should be appointed, despite Barlow's having been "elected a member of the French Convention": and "even admitted, I take it, to French citizenship."[12] Hamilton persisted but found that he could not persuade the Federalists in Philadelphia to change their minds about Madison. Adams and Hamilton did not write or see each other, and neither realized that the other was also urging Madison's appointment.

As rumors of Madison's appointment proliferated, surprisingly few Republicans considered the possibility seriously. James Fenno, publisher of *Gazette of the United States*, broached the idea of Madison's appointment after several conversations with Adams; but editor Benjamin Franklin Bache, of the rival *Aurora,* dismissed the suggestion. Unlike many others, the Duke de la Rochefoucauld-Laincourt, who had close ties with the Republicans, reported to France that Madison's selection was to be expected. Charles Maurice de Tallyrand-Périgord, soon to be named French minister of foreign affairs, suggested to an American that Madison would be an ideal choice for minister to France.[13] It has long been assumed that Adams had abandoned his plan to placate the Republicans by Madison's appointment following his approach to Jefferson. It is clear, however, that Adams refused to dismiss these hopes until defeated by his cabinet in late May at which time he settled upon the appointment of Charles C. Pinckney, Francis Dana, and John Marshall.

As reports of ship captures in the West Indies arrived daily, Adams began a comprehensive review of the entire crisis. On 19 March 1797 he asked all cabinet members for suggestions, acting on the assumption that the French had not accepted Pinckney's credentials. Before they could reply, Pinckney's first official dispatches arrived in New York and, on 22 March, were sent to Philadelphia.[14] The president received them on 24 March, finding the news worse than anticipated. Pinckney had been expelled from France and threatened with arrest. The United States had been denied the rights of embassy. Adams reacted quickly but deliberately; on 25 March he called a special session of Congress for 15 May.[15]

Adams then had to decide on the precise nature of his response to French actions. Not questioning the wisdom of renewed negotiations, he sought to combine negotiation with an expanded program of defense. By 8 April, James McHenry had prepared a program calling for a much-strengthened naval defense, harbor fortifications, and increases in the army and militia. Only by these defensive measures could the United States impress the French with the seriousness of American intentions.[16]

By mid-April Adams asked members of the cabinet for their views in preparation for his forthcoming speech to Congress. The president outlined several points that he wanted to make during the address, the foremost being "Our national Faith is to be held Sacred and inviolable." No agreement can be made with the Directory "inconsistent with any Article or Articles of our Treaties with Great Britain or any other Power." Adams further expressed his disapproval of the "Levity and Frivolity with which Professions and declarations are publickly made of Attachment to foreign Nations," noting that an ambassador should have no such feeling "but that of Respect, regard, Esteem and Politeness to any Nation or Country but his own." The president wanted no "good wishes or delight in the French Revolution. It is a subject wholly out of our Sphere of Jurisdiction. We are not the judges of it."[17] Adams's conception of compromise with France demanded that this erstwhile ally accept the United States' definition of its obligations, its neutrality policy, and its commercial agreement with Great Britain.

Nowhere in his administration did he find anyone who questioned these assumptions or even hinted of the need for major modifications.

Adams received replies from his cabinet members within two weeks. They agreed on fundamental points, each assuming or asserting the desirability of negotiations. No one advocated war, but all urged an increase in American defenses. They gave the president little advice on any specific policy to prevent the capture of American ships, because this was assumed to be the primary object of negotiations. Attorney General Charles Lee added a suggestion, which was adopted, to allow the consular convention of 1788 with France to lapse in 1798 rather than try to resolve the conflicting interpretations the two governments gave it.[18]

Adams addressed Congress on 16 May, 1797, after postponing the speech for a day because Congress lacked a quorum. Although written primarily by Secretary of State Pickering, the speech followed the guidelines that Adams himself had indicated. The president promised negotiations and promised to submit the names of the new envoys to the Senate shortly. He urged strengthening defenses to demonstrate the firmness and unity needed to prevent war and at the same time preserve American dignity.

In this speech Adams revealed a characteristic tendency to sound more belligerent in public addresses than in private statements. Instead of employing the olive branch and the arrow simultaneously, he left an impression of pugnacity, an impression that would create added difficulties for the special envoys in Paris. In the section of the address describing Monroe's leaving Paris, Adams commented on Barras's speech in more belligerent tones than those he used in private.

The speech of the President [Barras] discloses sentiments more alarming than the refusal of a minister, because more dangerous to our independence and union; and at the same time studiously marked with indignities towards the Government of the United States. It evinces a disposition to separate the people of the United States from the Government; to persuade them that they have different affections, principles, and interests, from those of their fellow citizens, whom they themselves have chosen to manage their common concerns; and thus to produce divisions fatal to our peace.[19]

Adams then went on to accuse France of fomenting revolution in the United States, concluding on a note that was hardly compromising:

> To investigate the causes which have encouraged the attempt is not necessary; but to repel, by decided and united councils, insinuations so derogatory to the honor, and aggressions so dangerous to the constitution, union, and even independence of the nation, is an indispensable duty.

Jefferson found the tone of Adams's statements harsh and rightly feared that the speech would be injurious to negotiations. Hamilton and George Cabot, on the other hand, thought the president showed necessary firmness, and they condescendingly indicated their surprise at how well he had handled himself.[20] The speech drew favorable reactions from most quarters, but this was not translated into congressional enactment of the proposed defensive measures. The strong Federalist majority in the Senate followed the president's recommendations, but the House of Representatives not only balked at the size of the defense program but even questioned its necessity. Albert Gallatin predicted that the House would beat back the Federalists and force the administration to put the emphasis on negotiations rather than defense,[21] and he proved to be right.

On 29 May, or possibly 28 May, Adams called his cabinet together to select the envoy or envoys to go to France. Between March and May, discussion had centered primarily on whether Madison would be chosen, but then the status of Charles C. Pinckney started to assume more importance. To assuage the insults to Pinckney's honor and to redeem the national honor, most observers assumed that he would be renominated. The cabinet gave its assent to Pinckney but then decided to add two more envoys.[22] When Adams suggested Elbridge Gerry, however, a majority of the cabinet objected to his lukewarm Federalism.[23] Acquiescing, the president selected Francis Dana of Massachusetts, who had been his secretary and had then served on an abortive mission to Russia during the American Revolution. No one objected to Dana. The deliberations on the third appointment are uncertain but important. Following the questions he presented to his cabinet, Adams has listed in his notes six men from Virginia and Maryland. First was Madison, followed by John Marshall, who was chosen.[24] After failing to gain support for Gerry, Adams apparently saw the futility of nominating Madison and passed directly to Marshall, his second choice. In effect, the president had yielded to the cabinet in the selection of envoys, a step that gave the commission geographical but not political balance.

When the nominations of Pinckney, Dana, and Marshall were submitted to the Senate the next day, Jefferson reported to Madison that "Charles Lee consulted a member from Virginia to know whether Marshall would be agreeable. He named you as more likely to give satisfaction. The answer was 'nobody of Mr. Mad's way of thinking will be appointed.'"[25] This statement has often been cited to demonstrate the partisan nature of the selection process, but the quotation fails to reveal Adams's attempts until the very last to name at least one nationally known Republican to the commission. This conversation took place after the cabinet meeting at which Gerry had been rejected and the possibility of considering Madison eliminated, but Jefferson and most, if not all, Republicans did not realize this. Adams's efforts to name envoys friendly to France and acceptable to Republicans had been more persistent than his contemporaries or later historians acknowledged.

When Dana declined to serve, as both Adams and Pickering had expected, the president proposed Gerry's name again. This time the cabinet accepted the choice, although with reservations.[26] The Senate ratified the appointments, a few Republicans voting against Marshall and Pinckney and a larger number of Federalists opposing Gerry.[27] At least in the Senate, a solid majority supported Adams's nominations in the first two years of his term, but within the cabinet the president made compromises that greatly weakened his policy. Originally seeking increased defense expenditures and a balanced commission, he found himself with a partisan commission and only nominal increases for defense.

The instructions for the new envoys were not completed until early July.[28] Pickering was the primary author of directives that can be described as flexible and nonbelligerent. If possible, the envoys were to try to recover damages for American shipping losses, but, because of the French government's well-known financial problems, they were to avoid seeking a specific sum or immediate payment. Pickering proposed that a commission similar to the one established for the same purposes under the Jay Treaty might be agreed upon to determine the validity and extent of American claims. Such a step, if approved, would postpone payment for damages for at least one year and probably for three or four. Pickering advised that it would be difficult to induce France to admit violations of previous treaties and suggested that the envoys seek a clause absolving either country of responsibility. The underlying objective of the instructions was the preservation of American neutrality.

The ultimata, or *sine qua non*, of the instructions deserve special mention, as they reveal the kind of relationship as well as broad agreement existing between Adams and Hamilton at this time. The ultimata stipulated that there should be no violation of previous treaties—a point that Adams had steadfastly insisted upon—no loans to France, no violation of American neutrality, and, lastly, a reaffirmation of all previous treaties, which would have included the Treaty of Alliance with France of 1778. As the instructions were drafted, James McHenry passed Hamilton's ideas along to Adams. Despite his many claims to the contrary after 1800, Adams knowingly drew on Hamilton's suggestions, condensing the latter's points to the four ultimata included in the instructions. On the top of his draft, Adams wrote, "H ideas."[29]

The president's acceptance of Hamilton's suggestions and his efforts to incorporate varying viewpoints mark him as one of the most accommodating men in his administration. What happened when James Monroe arrived in Philadelphia in late June offers the best example of how the French issue had divided men and parties. To his Federalist opponents Monroe was a symbol of servile fawning on France. He had been recalled in disgrace, and was constantly pilloried in the Federalist press. Explaining his position to the leaders in the Republican party, Jefferson, Albert Gallatin, and Aaron Burr, Monroe contended that, despite his own government's lack of support, he had attempted to justify Jay's Treaty to the Directory. Given time, he believed, the individual problems between France and the United States might have been resolved, leading to eventual French acceptance of the Jay Treaty. But his summary replacement by Pinckney and the subsequent break in relations between the two countries would make the task next to impossible.[30]

Monroe's speculations on the situation were self-serving but not completely erroneous. He had no opportunity to present his ideas or knowledge to the Federalists after his return. Timothy Pickering, who perhaps represented the worst of latter-day puritanism, immediately began to harass Monroe publicly about his accounts, his performance in France, and his politics. Hamilton accused Monroe of lacking honor as a gentleman even as he himself was fabricating documents for self-defense in an adultery scandal with Maria Reynolds. As he often did in political debates, Hamilton challenged Monroe to a duel.[31] A few days after Monroe's return to Philadelphia, John Marshall arrived to await final instructions before leaving for France, but he and Monroe had disagreed about French policy, and he did not see his friend of over a decade.[32] Even Washington took special pains to vent his hostility to Monroe, while Adams declared him as "dull heavy and Stupid a fellow as he could be consistently with Malignity and Inveteracy perpetual."[33] Whatever his failings, Monroe was the American the French government trusted most, and his information on French leaders was more accurate than that of any other leader in Philadelphia. His arguments about gaining acceptance of the Jay Treaty were not so much ignored as unheard by the Federalists in 1797.

The controversy surrounding Monroe suggests the character of what passed for debate on French policy in 1797. The issue was often whether someone was pro- or anti-French, not the kind of policy that the administration should pursue if it was to resolve the differences with the Directory. In the 1790s a person's political reference point was of fundamental importance. For many Federalists, political reliability was measured by an individual's support for the Constitution in 1787-1788. Thus, Charles C. Pinckney was acceptable and Elbridge Gerry unacceptable, because the South Carolinian had supported the Constitution, while the Massachusetts man had opposed ratification. John Marshall, the youngest and least experienced of the three envoys, had gained stature from Federalists and enmity from Republicans by denouncing Citizen Genet and defending the Jay Treaty.

For John Adams, Elbridge Gerry, and Charles Pinckney, however, the events of 1787 rarely seemed as critical as those of 1776 in evaluating a man's politics. To them the words republicanism, union, public duty, and partisanship referred to the 1770s, as Adams's unsuccessful overture to Jefferson in March 1797 and his strong support of Gerry demonstrate. Reflecting the partisan character of the decade of the 1790s, Marshall wrote on the day he swore Jefferson in as president that he believed him to be a terrorist.[34]

Of the new envoys Marshall was the first to accept appointment. A rising lawyer, skilled in his practice, and concerned with the place of law in society, Marshall had been offered cabinet positions under Washington. He refused these appointments, waiting to complete arrangements for the purchase of millions of acres of Fairfax lands in northern Virginia. He had also refused the position of minister to France, which Pinckney had accepted in 1795. But this time Marshall accepted the appointment within a week of his Senate confirmation.[35]

Gracious and friendly, Marshall rarely made bitter personal enemies, with the exception of Jefferson. He was a serious man, who in his letters from Europe rarely mentioned cultural affairs but spoke rather of taxation, governmental structure, and the relation of government to society.[36] Because Republicans considered Marshall pro-English, the Francophile St. George Tucker was surprised to find on Marshall's departure from Richmond "that of all *t'other Side Men* that I know he appears to me to preserve the best disposition to conciliate & preserve our pacific relations with France."[37] Marshall had sound political reasons for wanting peace with France, as can be seen in a personal letter that he had printed in the Richmond paper.

Has Virginia no sense of national honor? Is she so infatuated as not to perceive how rapidly she is meeting the horrors of St. Domingo? That from them, in case of war, nothing can save her but the northern states, and if Virginia prefers France to them, what inducements can they have to make

Figure 1. John Marshall by an unknown artist in Paris, 1797. *Courtesy of Mrs. Benjamin T. Woodruff.*

exertions for her? Another war in America will not be conducted with regard to the blacks as the former was, and they who think so, forget the change which has taken place of later years with respect to the rights of man.[38]

Elbridge Gerry was the most controversial of the appointments, and in his independent course in the XYZ affair he certainly justified his reputation. A merchant and early patriot in Massachusetts, he signed the Declaration of Independence and served repeatedly in the Continental Congress and then in the first federal Congress. Of the three envoys Gerry had the greatest political experience and public recognition. He was one of those rare men who believed that he could constantly disagree with associates over political issues and yet retain their friendship. His opponents, of whom there were a number, called Gerry "His Oddity."

Gerry reentered politics in 1796, casting an electoral vote for John Adams. He remained so unaffected by partisan conflict that he advised Jefferson that he should be happy to serve with Adams and wait to become president.[39] Gerry went out of his way to renew his correspondence with James Monroe and disapproved of his recall from France. He continued corresponding with Adams as well as Jefferson, showing a seeming innocence of the political hostility developing in the United States in 1797.[40] Politically Gerry was anti-British, or perhaps simply anti-George III.

Gerry accepted the appointment as envoy without reservation. He considered himself a special instrument to prevent war between the two republics, although he had no special sentimental attachment to France.[41] Gerry began the mission holding the advantage —extremely rare among politicians—of not having fought a political battle with John Adams in twenty years of public life. Of the two men Adams had greater prominence but in the influence of personality on political outlook and style they had remarkable similarities.

The third member of the delegation was Charles C. Pinckney, who had been so abruptly dismissed by the French government earlier in the year. Because he had waited for years for a diplomatic appointment, Pinckney did not sail immediately for home but went to The Hague and patiently waited for seven months for further instructions.[42] Pinckney had fought in the American Revolution and then had become a wealthy lawyer in Charleston. He was a member of the Constitutional Convention, and he and his relatives were among those South Carolina leaders consistently identified with the Federalist party.

A man of stern rectitude but pleasant manner, Pinckney felt strongly about the defense of American honor. He was a passionate nationalist rather than a republican, and his two years in Europe had reenforced his nationalism. Learning of his reeapointment, Pinckney exclaimed in characteristic Federalist rhetoric of the day that "a spirit of Union & Independence now pervades America. We shall soon have neither a British or a French faction there, nor suffer any foreigners to intermeddle in our affairs."[43] But as Pinckney was to learn to his chagrin, such a description would not even apply to both his colleagues in the coming months in Paris.

Notes

1. Alexander DeConde, *The Quasi-War* (New York, 1966), pp. 13-16; Manning J. Dauer, *The Adams Federalists*, 2d ed. (Baltimore, 1968), pp. 124-26; Ralph Ketcham, *James Madison* (New York, 1971,), pp. 367-68. Thomas Jefferson later recalled that Adams wanted a commission composed of Charles C. Pinckney, Elbridge Gerry, and James Madison, but it is clear that Jefferson must have written this after Pinckney and Gerry had been nominated. Franklin B. Sawvel, ed., *The Complete Anas of Thomas Jefferson* (New York, 1970), pp. 184-85.

2. Notes, 12 Mar.-13 Oct., 1797, inserted 10 May, 1797, Thomas Jefferson Papers, Library of Congress, Washington, D.C.

3. Dauer, *Adams Federalists*, pp. 96-97; Albert Bowman, *The Struggle for Neutrality* (Knoxville, 1974), pp. 262-78: Page Smith, *John Adams*, 2 vols. (New York, 1962) 2: 899, 112, 113.

4. Thomas Jefferson to Peter Carr, 12 April 1798, Jefferson Papers.

5. Alexandre Hauterive to Pierre Adet, 29 May 1797. Correspondance Politique, États-Unis, Supplement 2, Archives du Ministère des Affaires Étrangères, Paris (hereafter cited as Corr. Pol.).

6. John Adams to Abigail Adams, 13 January 1797, Adams Family Papers, Massachusetts Historical Society, Boston; Pierre Adet to Charles Delacroix, 28 November 1796, in *Correspondence of the French Ministers*, ed. Frederick J. Turner (Washington, D.C., 1904), pp. 978-80:

Jefferson to Madison, 22 January 1797, Madison Papers. Library of Congress, Washington, D.C.; Adet to Talleyrand, 22 September 1797, Corr. Pol., Vol. 48.

7. Adams to Elbridge Gerry, 30 May 1797, Conarroe Papers, Historical Society of Pennsylvania, Philadelphia.

8. Ibid.: quote from Adams to Abigail Adams, 18 January 1797, Adams Papers.

9. William Stinchcombe, *The American Revolution and the French Alliance* (Syracuse, 1969), pp. 153-59; Adams to Gerry, 26 August 1785. Knight-Gerry Papers, Massachusetts Historical Society, Boston, Massachusetts. For Adams's convenient, and quite opposite, use of the party label, see Adams to Gerry, 30 May 1797, Conarroe Papers; quote is from Adams to Abigail Adams, 18 December 1796, Adams Papers.

10. George Billias, *Elbridge Gerry* (New York, 1976), pp. 249-51; Winslow Watson, ed., *Memoirs of Elkanah Watson* (New York, 1856), pp. 345-46.

11. Wolcott definitely opposed appointing Madison, but the story that he threatened resignation was not related until much later. Oliver Wolcott, Jr., to Alexander Hamilton, 31 March 1797, in *The Papers of Alexander Hamilton*, 26 vols., ed. Harold Syrett et al. (New York, 1961-1979), 20: 569-74; John Adams to *Boston Patriot*, 29 May 1809; Jefferson, Notes, 10 May 1797 dates the time of his conversation as 6 March 1797, Jefferson Papers.

12. Quotes from Alexander Hamilton to William L. Smith, 5 April 1797, Smith to Hamilton, 1 May 1797, Pickering to Hamilton, 29 April 1797, *Papers of Hamilton* 21: 20-21, 75-76, 68-71. For other examples of Hamilton's sustained campaign to nominate Madison or Jefferson, see Hamilton to George Washington, [25-31] January 1797, to Rufus King, [15 February 1797], to Theodore Sedgwick, [26 February 1797], to Timothy Pickering, [22 March 1797], from Pickering, 26 March 1797, to Oliver Wolcott, Jr., [30 March 1797], from Oliver Wolcott, Jr., [31 March 1797], to James McHenry, [March 1797], to Oliver Wolcott, Jr., [5 April 1797], from McHenry [14 April 1797], to Pickering [11 May 1797], in ibid., 20: 480-82, 515-16; 521-22, 545-47, 548-49, 567-68, 569-74, 574-75; 21: 22-23, 48-49, 81-84.

13. John Fenno to Joseph Ward, 17 April 1797, Ward Family Papers, Chicago Historical Society, Chicago, Illinois; Philadelphia *Aurora*, 30 January 1797; LaRochefoucauld-Laincourt to Talleyrand, March 1797, Jean Marchand, ed., *Journal de Voyage en Amérique et d'un sojour à Philadelphie* (Baltimore and Paris, 1940), pp. 145-48; for Talleyrand, see James Pitcairn to John Q. Adams, October 1796, Adams Papers.

14. Memorandum, 19 March 1797, Adams Papers; LeRoy, Bayard, and McEvers to P. & C. Van Eeghen, 23 March 1797, Holland Land Company Papers, Vol. 153, Gemeentearchief, Amsterdam.

15. *Aurora*, 25 March 1797; Marvin Zahniser, *Charles Cotesworth Pinckney* (Chapel Hill, 1967), pp. 141-49; Adams to Abigail Adams, 27 March 1797, Adams Papers; cf. DeConde, *Quasi-War*, p. 383.

16. Estimates on Defensive Needs, 8 April 1797, Adams Papers.

17. Instructions & Speech; minutes to be asked of Secretaries, [April 1797], ibid.

18. For the cabinet members' replies, see under 30 April 1797 and 1 May 1797 (two by Pickering) and 5 May 1797, ibid.; Bernard Steiner, *Life and Correspondence of James McHenry* (Cleveland, 1907), pp. 213-23; George Gibbs, Jr., *The Administrations of Washington and Adams*, 2 vols. (New York, 1846), 1: 502-17.

19. *Debates and Proceedings in the Congress of the United States, 1789-1825* (Washington, 1834-1856), 16 May 1797, 7: 54-59 (hereafter, *Annals.*)

20. Jefferson to ———, 29 May 1797, Jefferson Papers; for Hamilton, see Bowman, *Struggle for Neutrality,* p. 283; for Cabot, Smith, *Adams*, 2: 931.

21. Albert Gallatin to James Nicholson, 26 May 1797, Gallatin Papers, New-York Historical Society, New York, New York.

22. Questions to be proposed [29 May 1797], Adams Papers, filed under the date of October 1797; the date was probably the 29th, because Jefferson still believed that only Pinckney would be nominated, Jefferson to ———, 29 May 1797, Jefferson Papers.

23. For the controversy, see James McHenry to Timothy Pickering, 23 February 1811, in Henry C. Lodge, *Life and Times of George Cabot* (Boston, 1878), p. 204; Gibbs, *Washington and Adams,* 1: 467, 469, 471; for important Adams letters see Gibbs, *Washington and Adams*, 1: 462, 465; 2: 191, 192, 197, 205, 209, 221, 223, 269, 271n, 277. Timothy Pickering, *A Review of the Correspondence between the Honorable John Adams and the Late William Cunningham, Esq.* (Salem, 1824), pp. 79-80. For a contemporary account, see Adams to Gerry, 20 June 1797, Adams Papers.

24. The other names were Ludwell Lee, Thomas Lee, Bushrod Washington, and William Vans Murray.

25. Jefferson to Madison, 1 June 1797, Madison Papers.

26. Pickering to Charles C. Pinckney, 1 June 1797, Timothy Pickering Papers, Massachusetts Historical Society, Boston, Massachusetts; Abigail Adams to Mary Cranch, 3 June 1797, Adams Papers.

27. The Senate approved Pinckney's nomination by a twenty-to-four vote, Marshall and Dana by a vote of twenty-two to six and Gerry by twenty-one to six. 5 June and 22 June 1797, "Records of the United States;" "Records of Executive Proceedings;" "Executive Nominations and Accompanying Papers," Record Group 46, National Archives; Washington, D.C.

28. Pickering to American Envoys, 15 July 1797, "Instructions to United States Ministers," 1, Record Group 59, National Archives, Washington, D.C.

29. Instructions, "H Ideas," Undated, Reel 387, Adams Papers.

30. Albert Gallatin to Hannah Gallatin, 28 June 1797, Gallatin Papers.

31. *Papers of Hamilton*, 21: Introductory note, pp. 121-44, and 144-288 *passim*; for a brilliant exposition of the partisan nature of the affair and the role of Hamilton as well as Jefferson and Monroe, see Julian Boyd, ed., *The Papers of Thomas Jefferson*, 19 vols. to date (Princeton, N.J., 1950-), 18: 611-88.

32. Harry Ammon, *James Monroe* (New York, 1971), pp. 81-82.

33. James Flexner, *George Washington*, 4 vols. (Boston, 1965-1972), 289-92; 383; quote from Adams to Gerry, 30 May 1797, Conarroe Papers.

34. John Marshall to Charles C. Pinckney, 4 March 1801, Pinckney Family Papers, Library of Congress, Washington, D.C.

35. George Washington to Timothy Pickering, 8 July 1796, Washington Papers, Library of Congress, Washington, D.C.

36. John Marshall to Edward Carrington, 2 September 1797, Morristown National Historical Park, Morristown, New Jersey; to George Washington, 15 September 1797, Washington Papers; to Charles Lee, 22 September 1797, Emmet Collection, New York Public Library, New York.

37. St. George Tucker to John Page, 23 June 1797, William C. Stinchcombe and Charles T. Cullen, eds., *The Papers of John Marshall* 3 vols. (Chapel Hill, 1979), 3: 81.

38. Charles Lee to John Marshall, c. 5 May 1797, *ibid.*, p. 72.

39. Elbridge Gerry to Thomas Jefferson, 4 and 13 May 1797; Jefferson to Gerry, 13 May 1797, Jefferson Papers.

40. Ibid. Gerry to James Monroe, 23 July 1797, Monroe Papers, Library of Congress, Washington, D.C.; Gerry to John Adams, 27 March 1797; Gerry to Abigail Adams, 28 December 1796, Adams Papers.

41. Elbridge Gerry to William Vans Murray, 28 December 1797, Gratz Collection, Historical Society of Pennsylvania, Philadelphia.

42. Charles Pinckney to James Madison, 6 August 1791, Madison Papers.

43. Charles Pinckney to Joseph Pitcairn, 15 June 1797, Joseph Pitcairn Papers, Cincinnati Historical Society, Cincinnati, Ohio.

3

"War Leads to No Useful Result"

French policy toward the United States changed monthly during the revolution's upheavals in 1797. A weak five-man Directory found itself increasingly dependent on military power and under attack by a small group in the lower legislative chamber, the Council of Five Hundred. Led by Emmanuel de Pastoret, critics castigated the Directory for its policy toward the republican governments of Geneva, Venice, and the United States. These critics were not pro-American, however, or even pro-republican; their purpose was to gain greater power for the legislative branch of government.[1] To stave off any diminution of its power, the Directory in June responded by dismissing four ministers, including the anti-American foreign minister Charles Delacroix. A compromise within the Directory allowed Paul Barras to advance his own candidate, Charles M. de Talleyrand-Périgord, for foreign minister.

After almost four years of exile in Great Britain and the United States, Talleyrand had returned home to France in the fall of 1796. He had been a candidate for the Assembly and the Directory but had failed to gain election. The foreign office was his first ministerial position in a career that would span almost four decades, but he had yet to develop the power that he would enjoy under Napoleon and the Restoration. Since 1791 the office of foreign minister had been a precarious position; including the period in which the foreign office was directed by a commission under the Committee of Public Safety, there had been at least fourteen incumbents. Of these, five had been killed, four were in exile in 1797, and at least two others had been imprisoned at some time during the previous six years. [2]

The politics of foreign policy revolved around battles for internal dominance as well as increasing rivalry among military leaders. Unsure of his political strength in this situation and still a symbol of the constitutional royalists, whom he had once supported, Talleyrand complained privately that the Directory treated him more as an errand boy than a minister. He could direct the foreign office but not the French foreign policy. The Prussian minister to France, Sandoz Rollin, informed his government that Talleyrand had little or no influence on European policy, which remained under Director Jean Reubell's watchful eye. [3] Only in policy toward the United States could Talleyrand operate relatively free of interference.

Many Americans viewed the choice of Talleyrand as a good omen for French-American relations. [4] The new foreign minister had lived in the United States from 1794 to 1796, and his acquaintance with American customs and government exceeded that of most Frenchmen. Joseph Pitcairn, a New York merchant and Paris neighbor of Talleyrand, remarked that Talleyrand "has for us many advantages over his predecessor—he is superior in natural talents and in acquired—but above all he knows America and particularly her leading men very well." [5]

During his time in the United States, Talleyrand had considered the commercial and diplomatic relations between the New World and Europe. He had prepared papers for Theophile Cazenove, head of the Holland Land Company in the United States, on the sale of American land to Europeans. [6] Following his return to Paris in September 1796, he was elected to the second section of the Institut National, dedicated to the moral and philosophical sciences. Talleyrand had delivered two papers, "Commercial Relations of the United States with England" and "An Essay upon the Advantages to be derived from New Colonies." [7] In these papers Talleyrand sought to isolate a nation's true interests, its commercial patterns, and its ties of culture and language. From the enduring bonds established by a common language and heritage followed commercial connections.

Talleyrand returned repeatedly to English success in trade with the United States after the American Revolution. Practical reasons underlying English manufacturing and the growth of an American agricultural society complemented and cemented the advantages offered by common laws and language. "Americans," he wrote, "find themselves Englishmen," and the open land available in the United States had helped to dissipate the hostility to England caused by the American War of Independence.[8] Now the English and Americans traded more than before the war, had a common, if not joint, policy on American expansion into the Mississippi Valley, and found themselves connected more by interest than by any alliance. Conversely, Talleyrand noted, the same phenomenon could be seen in Louisiana and Canada. Although the Spanish and English had ruled those areas for more than thirty years, in each colony there was a bias toward France. Common language and culture were again predominant.[9] France now faced a problem in its colonies because the British had superiority on the seas and a revolt was underway in Haiti. Although Talleyrand did not say so explicitly, he saw relations there as identical to those between Great Britain and the United States. In 1795 Talleyrand had written, "Whatever changes occur in the government of France it will not for long be in the power of anyone to subject to labor the workers who have tasted independence."[10] In his second speech before the Institut National Talleyrand spoke of new colonies and foresaw the independence of the West Indian possessions. He suggested Egypt and colonies on the coast of Africa as replacements for the anticipated and, to him, inevitable loss of the West Indian islands.[11]

The Antilles would have natural reciprocal relations with the United States, but Talleyrand expressed little fear over a loss of commerce, because by his analysis, ties of habit, language, and culture would remain after independence. Talleyrand did not have an enlightened view of commerce or a commitment to free trade as a liberating influence, for he was really not concerned with this point. The fact of revolution leading to independence in the New World had changed and would change the form but not the reality of diplomatic and commercial relations. Talleyrand was quite prepared to consider retaking Louisiana or founding other colonies, but he wished to avoid the mistakes that had created independence movements or saddled France with a heavy financial burden. By no means did he wish to return to the colonial policy of the ancien régime but, rather, to base a new policy on free emigration patterns allowing adequate economic opportunity to new French settlers.

Despite his interest in America, Talleyrand realized that the United States represented a significant problem for French policy. Members of the Directory did not regard American neutrality favorably. Talleyrand, however, feared that if the United States were to abandon neutrality, it would ally itself with Great Britain, but this did not seem an immediate prospect. During his first assignment in Paris, Charles C. Pinckney had reported that Talleyrand described America as not of greater "consequence to them [the Directory] nor ought it to be treated with greater respect than Geneva or Genoa." [12] But after analyzing Talleyrand's speeches, John Q. Adams concluded that the record was not as unfavorable to the United States as this quotation suggested. Talleyrand, he wrote, "was better disposed than many persons have represented him, and I have believed that pains were taken to misrepresent him to Mr. P[inckney] while he was in Paris." [13]

As the new foreign minister, Talleyrand could not undertake drastic staff changes, but in the few appointments he made in his first months of office he favored men he had known in the United States or others who had previously dealt with Americans. In charge of funding he placed Charles de la Forest, who had held minor diplomatic posts in the United States almost continuously from 1779 to 1794. Alexandre Hauterive, consul at New York and a longtime acquaintance of Talleyrand, returned to France in 1797 and immediately began to analyze American politics for the foreign ministry. Hauterive accepted an official post within the ministry in 1798. [14] A holdover who was retained in office under Talleyrand was Louis Pichon, who had served in the French embassy in Philadelphia in 1794-1795. Pichon continued in the section of the foreign office that handled American affairs and later served as a contact with William V. Murray, the American minister to the Netherlands, after the collapse of negotiations in 1798. One of Talleyrand's private secretaries, Louis Paul d'Autremont, had lived in Asylum, Pennsylvania, before returning to France with Talleyrand in 1796. [15] The two previous ministers to the United States, Joseph Fauchet and Pierre Adet, both awaiting reassignment, also commented on United States policy, as did Louis Otto, whose experience in the United States began during the American Revolution. Within a year, Talleyrand gave Otto his first permanent diplomatic assignment in almost four years.

Through these appointments Talleyrand sought to restore the professional standing of a diplomatic corps, which was still shaken by the events of 1791-1795. He may have also preferred diplomats who had served in a republican country to counteract frequent charges that former royalists received favor under the Directory and in his ministry. In any case, when Talleyrand needed advice on United States policy, he could draw on a number of men with informed opinions.

In the summer and fall of 1797 six reports were submitted to Talleyrand in anticipation of French-American negotiations. These reports reflected the changes that had taken place in relations between the two countries since the outbreak of war with Great Britain in 1793. Of papers written by Adet, Fauchet, Hauterive, and Otto, and two by an anonymous author (perhaps Pichon), only Otto's recalled the familiar but now time-worn theme of mutual struggle against England during the American Revolution.[16] To Otto, the American government had shown abiding friendship for France by paying off its debt obligations ahead of schedule, never breaking diplomatic ties, even during the Reign of Terror, and continuing to express sympathy for France and the French Revolution. Otto neglected the events of 1796 and 1797, attributing strained diplomatic relations for the maladroit actions of successive French ministers in Philadelphia. Otto's paper was more appropriate to an earlier period of French-American relations when many Frenchmen believed that the United States should hold a special position in French policy, a position no longer accepted by either Talleyrand or the Directory.[17]

The authors of the other reports agreed on the fundamental issues of contention between the two countries. They argued that French-American relations had been deteriorating since the arrival of the French minister Edmond Genet in Philadelphia in 1793. Coinciding with Genet's arrival, moreover, came President Washington's proclamation of neutrality without prior consultation with French officials. This was the first indication of a new status for France in American foreign policy. Washington's later request for the recall of Genêt merely continued this new American policy. Most important of all, the agreement by the United States to the treaty negotiated by John Jay in 1794 marked the culminating step in an increasingly hostile American policy toward France. The subsequent ratification of the Jay Treaty by the United States Senate in 1795 and the appropriation of funds to implement it by the House of Representatives the next year made it apparent that the break between the two republics reflected more than the machinations of a few members of an anti-French faction in the Washington administration. As the authors assessed American policy, especially by the time of the Jay Treaty's ratification, they grudgingly acknowledged that a change of one or two men in key positions, even the presidency, would not substantially alter the policy of the United States.

Nevertheless, the French diplomats agreed, the United States had openly violated both the letter and the spirit of its previous treaties with France when it approved the Jay Treaty. The authors could suggest no effective remedy to counteract the treaty's pernicious effects. One proposal called for the United States to renounce the Jay Treaty, a recommendation that Talleyrand rejected out of hand in a margin note, because, he noted, it imposed too great an indignity on a sovereign nation.[18] A more complicated tactic to achieve the same end would be to renegotiate the definition of contraband so as to nullify the interpretation agreed to by the United States in Jay's Treaty.[19] By following the latter strategy, it was argued, France could demonstrate its willingness to negotiate while causing an inevitable increase in tension between the United States and Great Britain.

Seeing the problem from the French viewpoint, the authors postulated, rather optimistically, that the United States would be at a disadvantage in the forthcoming negotiations. The glaring inconsistency between the French Commercial Treaty of 1778 and the Jay Treaty would provide, they hoped, the opportunity of placing the burden of treaty violations squarely on the Americans.[20] The guarantee clause of the defensive treaty of 1778, which stipulated that the United States would guarantee French West Indian possessions, was a standing obligation of the United States, and this clause could be used as a cudgel with which to compel the Americans to compromise on other issues, particularly maritime questions, if the American envoys sought to persuade France to renounce the guarantee article. The French analysts further assumed that the Americans' major demand would be for an indemnity for the losses suffered at the hands of French privateers, but this France could parry by stressing United States obligations and violations of the commercial treaty.[21] Exactly how this was to be accomplished remained understandably vague, but French diplomats hoped that by tactical measures they could counteract the expected American emphasis on apparent French violations at sea.

The analysts did not ignore France's vulnerability in the approaching negotiations, however. They assumed—and some stated flatly—that France had also violated the treaties of 1778. No author argued that the capture of United States ships was legal or that France was not liable for damages. In fact, one author urged that the government make a major effort to get exact figures on the number of captures in order to counter expected American claims, and this was done.[22] Moreover, to strengthen the French position, the Directory would have to revise its policies to bring them into accord with the Commercial Treaty of 1778.[23] The first change called for repeal of the *Arrête* of July 1796, which declared that France would treat all neutrals as they suffered Great Britain to treat them. This policy had been adopted by the Directory partly as a retaliatory measure against American acceptance of Jay's Treaty. The other issue concerned the recently enacted requirement that American ships entering French ports carry a *role d'équipage*, essentially a cargo and crew manifest, signed by a French consular official. Under this requirement a number of American ships had already been seized and condemned. None of the writers saw the *role d'équipage* requirement as more than a political tactic, and some advised that it should be abandoned whenever the need arose.

The substance of these reports indicated that France, more than the United States, needed to change its policy to comply with the treaties of 1778. Although the authors left this conclusion unstated, they realized that France would not have a clear-cut legal position if it relied heavily on the treaties of 1778. Not surprisingly, Talleyrand deliberately diverted the negotiations from this issue and into other directions in the following six months.

American leaders considered tensions between the two countries to be far more serious than did their French counterparts, and Americans insisted that if French maritime attacks continued, war would probably erupt.[24] French diplomats, on the other hand, did not think the situation nearly so ominous, and although they recommended stopping the attacks, they did not consider war the alternative. The question of possible war was mentioned only to be dismissed as an absurdity.[25] The French analysts could see no political goal that would justify war with the United States. If war did break out, they pointed out, supplies to the French West Indian colonies would be cut off, and the United States would probably enter into virtual alliance with Great Britain. The primary purpose of French policy should remain as it had been since 1778, to lessen American dependence on Great Britain. War would only increase the dependence and perhaps make it permanent.

The reports submitted to Talleyrand virtually ignored the newly appointed American envoys and concentrated instead on John Adams. The authors offered more sophisticated assessment of Adams than previous French interpretations. No one returned to the oft-told circumstances of Adams's well-known jealousy of Benjamin Franklin or of Adams's reputed perfidy to France and partiality to Great Britain in the 1782 peace negotiations. Louis Otto excepted, the French diplomats expected that Adams would be more accommodating to France than Washington had been. Otto's beliefs, unchanged since 1790, reflected a Lafayette-like veneration of Washington as well as an intense dislike of Adams.[26] Obviously Adams had not been the preferred choice for the presidency, as seen by Adet's efforts to assist Jefferson's election in 1796, but since becoming president, Adams had given unmistakable indications that he wanted to prevent war with France.[27]

No French official who studied American politics deluded himself about Adams's detestation for the French government, however. But Adams's close victory over Jefferson, according to the French view, would inhibit the inclinations of his many anti-French advisers. Given the disunity in the United States caused by the Jay Treaty and the presidential race, it was correctly predicted that Adams could not and would not take decisive steps to alienate France further.[28] Instead, the domestic political situation would force him, whatever his personal feelings, to work for a resolution of the problems with France.

The contents of the reports written for Talleyrand are also significant for what they omit. No one suggested that France should depend on the Republican party in the United States to achieve French aims. Jefferson, Madison, Monroe, and other Republican leaders received no mention. Nor did any writer identify a French party in the United States, although opposition to French policy continued to be considered the work of a British party. The only analyst even to mention the Republican party commented that it was depending on the French to remain conciliatory in the forthcoming negotiations but did not elaborate on this thought.[29] Despite the persistent suspicions of American leaders, French specialists on America did not think it either wise or profitable to depend on current political divisions in the United States for the achievement of French policy. To most Federalists and to the American envoys in Paris, however, it became an article of faith to regard the French as deliberately fomenting dissent within the United States to serve their own purposes.[30] French officials could surely see advantages for France in the conflict between the American parties, but they needed to do nothing to promote it. American political divisions would help France only insofar as they would probably prevent an openly anti-French policy by the Adams administration. Beyond this, the French analysts agreed, American domestic considerations offered a weak basis for long-range policy.

The connection between policy toward the United States and French colonial objectives also received only brief mention. The French West Indies warranted comment only to emphasize their dependence on the United States for foodstuffs.[31] Hauterive alone referred to Louisiana in connection with the French Caribbean possessions.[32] He advocated, as had numerous Frenchmen since 1763, that France reacquire Louisiana to prevent American penetration to the Gulf of Mexico. Otto, who had strongly urged this policy in 1789, omitted the subject in 1797.[33] Hauterive wanted to establish a French colony in the Mississippi Valley to retard American and British expansion. Such a colony, he argued, could help supply foodstuffs to the West Indies, thereby lessening France's dependence on the United States in the Western Hemisphere.[34]

The most important and influential statement on French-American relations came in Talleyrand's culminating report, sent to the Directory for approval probably in the second week of October.[35] In the report, Talleyrand carefully reviewed the origins of the division between the two countries, summarized the current status of negotiations, and recommended future policy. He unquestionably drew upon the papers written under his direction while at the same time taking a broader view of the possible alternatives facing the Directory.

It is well to keep in mind when considering the negotiations with France in 1797-1798 Robert R. Palmer's observation that Talleyrand's "influence in these years hardly went beyond the writing of magisterial memoranda."[36] As discussed earlier, in most areas of French foreign policy Palmer's comment is justified, but the course of the American negotiations in the next nine months did develop from Talleyrand's original recommendations to the Directory in October 1797. Talleyrand advised proceeding slowly with the American negotiations, and much of his policy must be viewed in this light.[37] To prolong the negotiations, Talleyrand intended to request an explanation of President Adams's speech at the opening of Congress on 16 May 1797, a statement that the French considered insolent. Talleyrand stressed that such an explanation must not be considered an apology by the Americans but simply recognition that France would not negotiate when threatened. If the American envoys met this initial demand appropriately, then the Directory should indicate a willingness to enter formal negotiations on all substantive issues.[38]

The approach that Talleyrand outlined gave him a number of advantages. He did not have to ask the Directory to make a decision on a possible indemnity that France might have to pay to the United States. Furthermore, by pursuing this strategy, Talleyrand postponed consideration of the possible repeal of the *Arrête* of 12 July 1796 concerning neutral trade, a policy that violated the treaty of 1778. Instead of confronting the question directly, Talleyrand noted that because of the decree "our agents in the Colonies accordingly took certain measures which pressed heavily on American trade with the English Colonies."[39] Returning to this point a second time, Talleyrand indicated his position on the privateers in the West Indies by declaring that "the time has come to remove the despotic actions and violence which are carried out against the Americans in our Antilles," but again he refrained from requesting any immediate action by the Directory.[40]

The bribery attempt and loan requests made by Talleyrand's agents, Jean Hottinguer and Pierre Bellamy, to the American envoys within a week of the report's completion have been taken as an indication that venality dominated Talleyrand's thoughts.[41] Yet even before these demands Baron d'Osmond and later Louis d'Autremont, both secretaries to Talleyrand, and Caron de Beaumarchais made repeated requests to the Americans for some explanation of Adams's speech.[42] The extortion requests by Hottinguer and Bellamy first came after d'Osmond had informed the Americans of the necessity of an explanation, which the envoys refused to give.[43]

Even after the bribery demand was dropped and the loan request refused by the Americans, Talleyrand remained adamant in his insistence on an explanation as late as March 1798.[44] The issue of an explanation did not cause the collapse of negotiations, but at no time did the three American commissioners seriously consider making an explanation of Adams's critical comments on the French government. Indeed, they gave no thought as to why the French made this request so repeatedly. Instead, the American envoys agreed from the beginning of their stay in Paris that it was beneath the dignity of the United States to offer any explanation beyond a reiteration of Adams's conclusion that the United States would adhere to all existing agreements; even this assurance was not transmitted to the French government.[45] The Americans mistakenly associated the demand for an explanation with the bribe, assuming that the first demand provided a cover for the bribe and loan requests.[46] Talleyrand did indeed seek a bribe but later dropped the demand in the course of negotiations. Nevertheless, the one procedural point most consistently pressed by the French was for some kind of explanation of Adams's speech.

In his report Talleyrand had concluded that the primary source of errors in French policy between 1792 and 1797 had been misplaced confidence in the Washington administration. Despite numerous indications to the contrary, the French government had "stubbornly persisted in seeing friends in the American administration."[47] By placing unlimited confidence in the former American minister James Monroe, French leaders had failed to pay adequate attention to the negotiations between John Jay and Lord Grenville that resulted in Jay's Treaty. The faith in Monroe "was so implicit that we found it hard to believe in the treaty even when all the gazettes had announced it." Accordingly, Monroe's vast influence weakened the "sensation" caused by the news of the Jay Treaty's ratification. In a direct criticism of his predecessor, Charles Delacroix, Talleyrand concluded that France had been too hesitant, losing the immediate opportunity to impress upon the United States its anger and opposition to the treaty.

Talleyrand further contended that in his last two years in office Washington had not proposed any measures conciliatory to France. By recalling Monroe, Washington erroneously attributed responsibility to his minister's performance rather than acknowledging the Jay Treaty's effects. In his Farewell Address Washington had unmistakably, although indirectly, attacked French influence in the United States. Moreover, Washington's secretary of state, Timothy Pickering, had published a bitter attack on France in January 1797, alleging that France had tried to sabotage American aspirations in the peace negotiations of 1782. "It is in this manner," Talleyrand concluded, "that General Washington conducted himself in our behalf at the close of his political career."

The contrast between Washington and Adams could not have been greater, in Talleyrand's view. Adams would surely act cautiously because of his small electoral majority in 1796. Talleyrand made no mention of any contribution Jefferson might make to American policy, but went on to note that the president's first speeches and his appointment of the envoys demonstrated an interest in reconciliation between the two powers. Apparently Talleyrand saw no contradiction in finding Adams sincere in his desire for peace and belligerent in comments which required an explanation from the American envoys. Adams's prompt action in the Blount conspiracy, which involved a breakaway movement by frontier politicians led by Tennessee Senator William Blount, who had planned to attack Spanish territories with British backing, convinced Talleyrand that the new president would act decisively against the British party in the United States. More importantly Adams's actions suggested that he would not seek closer ties with

Great Britain. Adams's election, therefore, offered a basis for optimism about the prospects for accommodation between the two countries.

Talleyrand saw other events in the United States that seemed favorable to France. He detected a permanent breach between the government and the people, a conclusion he may have reached in the course of travels in the United States during the widespread protests against Jay's Treaty. Talleyrand further contended that Americans had repudiated Washington's proclamation of neutrality, as seen in the public receptions that Genet received. In opposition to the Washington administration, members of Congress had led the battle for an anti-British navigation act in 1793 and 1794. The short-lived embargo of 1794 was repealed not because of fear of British retaliatory measures but rather because Joseph Fauchet convinced congressional leaders that it was harmful to France. Talleyrand also reminded the Directory of the divisions in Congress, which had nearly rejected the Jay Treaty and by a solid majority refused to acquiesce to Adams's military and naval programs in 1797.

In describing American politics, Talleyrand exaggerated the division between Congress and the public on one side and the administration on the other. He did not, however, make the error common in both the United States and France of equating public opinion or Congress with the views of any political party. Nor did he assume that France's policy could be implemented by depending on French influence in the Republican party.

The question of how war or peace would affect the French West Indian colonies drew some of Talleyrand's strongest comments. He dismissed the practicality of war emphatically, because "First of all, war leads to no useful result." Furthermore, the colonies' peacetime dependence on the United States made it evident that France could not afford to alienate that country permanently. Instead, Talleyrand recommended that the rapidly developing reciprocal trade between the United States and the colonies be encouraged and no restrictions be reimposed on it in the future. His policy of seeking peace, not war, with the United States indicated wisdom rather than fear, Talleyrand counseled the Directory. The United States Navy would not be strong enough to take possession of any of the islands in the event of war, and, furthermore, the American public probably would not support such a costly venture, he added. Seen from the French side, war with the United States would undermine France's foreign policy in two critical areas: it would inevitably produce a closer political and financial relation between Great Britain and the United States, and it would severely damage France's ally, Spain.

Talleyrand found ample evidence of aggressive American intentions toward Spanish Louisiana. Americans had gladly cooperated with Genet in 1793 to launch attacks on Spanish possessions, and the Blount conspiracy in 1797 revealed that they would likewise cooperate with Great Britain to gain their objective. If war was not averted, the French would have no way to stop the Americans, who would probably join the British forces to overwhelm Spanish garrisons in the lower Mississippi Valley. Spain had obstinately rebuffed French pressures to cede Louisiana to France, which had the power to prevent an American victory. Talleyrand refrained from carrying his analysis to its logical conclusion and asked for an increased effort to convince Spain to transfer Louisiana to France, as specified in the Treaty of Basel in 1795. Again, as throughout his report, Talleyrand urged that colonial questions be subordinated to the more immediate concern of the continuing war with Great Britain. Such a policy made peaceful relations with the United States crucial.

British policy toward the United States, Talleyrand observed, had been uniformly hostile except in one critical area. Britain, it appeared, "had a marked interest in favoring the gradual spread of the American population," allowing the United States to gain the most desirable lands in the American West. Talleyrand explained this apparent anomaly by asserting that Great Britain's future prosperity depended on growing numbers of consumers for its manufacturing. By acquiescing to American expansion, Great Britain would reap commercial benefits from this increasing and largely agricultural population. By its very nature this policy would unquestionably aid and abet American designs on Louisiana.

Echoing his initial speech before the Institute, Talleyrand returned in his conclusion to the long-term prospects for continued friendship between the United States and France. The French could not expect Americans to renew the ties forged during the American Revolution, for the bonds of culture and language gave

Great Britain an insurmountable advantage over France. But reconciliation with the United States should be accomplished if only to limit the prospective damage to France and Spain. In the nonideological language characteristic of French officials when speculating on American affairs, Talleyrand advised the Directory, "Let us therefore see what utility demands at the moment. The measure of our future conduct must be that of our interests."[48]

If we compare Talleyrand's statement and the instructions given to the American envoys, we can see that the positions of the two governments were not far apart. Both wanted to prevent war, neither emphasized the French alliance of 1778 or its obligations, and both recognized an end to French maritime abuses as the key to improving diplomatic relations. Yet there was an important difference which prevented any substantive negotiations on outstanding issues for almost a year. French policy was predicated on lengthy negotiations, while the American envoys wanted to reach an agreement quickly to profit more fully from the American policy of neutrality.

Notes

1. Robert R. Palmer, *The Age of the Democratic Revolution*, 2 vols. (Princeton, N.J., 1964), 2: 255-60; Georges LeFebvre, *The French Revolution*, 4 vols., trans. John H. Stewart and James Frigulietti (New York, 1964), 2: 171-82, 197-99; Isser Woloch, *Jacobin Legacy* (Princeton, N.J., 1970), pp. 77, 364; Georgia Robison, *Revellière-Lépeaux, Citizen Director* (New York, 1938), p. 48.

2. Information gathered from Frédéric Masson, *Le Départment des Affaires Étrangères pendant la Révolution* (Paris, 1877), *passim*.

3. Sandoz Rollin dispatches, 13 August and 24 October 1797, in *Preussen und Frankreich von 1795 bis 1807: Diplomatische Correspondenzen*, 2 vols. ed. Paul Bailleu (Leipzig, 1881-1887), 1: 142-43, 155.

4. Gouverneur Morris to James Mountflorence, 18 August 1797, Gouverneur Morris Papers, vol. 24, Library of Congress, Washington, D.C. Robert Morris to Talleyrand, 8 January 1797, Robert Morris Papers, Library of Congress, Washington, D.C.; William L. Smith to Talleyrand, 8 November 1797, Smith Papers, vol. 1, Library of Congress, Washington, D.C.; Rufus King to Talleyrand, 3 August 1797, Rufus King Papers, vol. 43, New-York Historical Society, New York, New York.

5. Joseph Pitcairn to Rufus King, 3 August 1797, vol. 39, Rufus King Papers.

6. Hans Huth and Wilma Pugh, eds., *Talleyrand in America as a Financial Promoter,* American Historical Association Annual Report for 1941, 3 vols. (Washington, D.C., 1942). 2: 33-57, 110-15, 137-75.

7. The edition used here, including both speeches published as one pamphlet, is Charles M. Talleyrand, "Commercial Relations of the United States with England," 4 April 1797; "An Essay upon the advantages to be derived from New Colonies," 3 July 1797 (Boston, 1809); Georges LaCour-Gayet, *Talleyrand,* 4 vols. (Paris, 1930-1933), 1: 214-18.

8. Talleyrand, "Commercial Relations," p. 12.

9. Talleyrand, "An Essay on New Colonies," p. 20.

10. Huth and Pugh, eds., *Talleyrand in America,* p. 93.

11. Talleyrand, "An Essay on New Colonies," p. 21.

12. Charles C. Pinckney to Timothy Pickering, 20 December 1796, "Diplomatic Despatches, France" 5, Record Group 59, National Archives, Washington, D.C.

13. John Q. Adams to Joseph Pitcairn, 14 August 1797, Pitcairn Papers, Cincinnati Historical Society, Cincinnati, Ohio.

14. Masson, *Le Départment des Affaires Étrangères,* 406-08, 411, 472-73, 485, 489. Charles de la Forest had speculated in American lands while serving as a French consul in the United States. He named a son Blount Hawkins de la Forest, after Willam Blount and Benjamin Hawkins of North Carolina. See Benjamin Hawkins to William Blount, 30 January and 8 February 1790, Alice B. Keith, ed., *The John Gray Blount Papers,* 3 vols. (Raleigh, 1952-1965), 2: 8-10, 12-14. Hauterive was paid from secret funds to report on American affairs after Adet left his position.

15. William Rawle to Timothy Pickering, 31 October 1798, Pickering Papers, Massachusetts Historical Society, Boston; Theophile Cazenove report on Asylum Company, Holland Land Company Papers, vol. 268, Gemeentearchief, Amsterdam.

16. Louis Otto, "Considérations sur la Conduite du Gouvernement Américain envers la France, depuis le commencement de la Révolution jusqu'en 1797," June-July 1797, Correspondance Politique, États-Unis, vol. 48, Archives du Ministère des Affaires Étrangères, Paris, (hereafter Corr. Pol.); Joseph Fauchet, *A Sketch of the Present State of Our Political Relations with the United States of North America* (Philadelphia, 1797), dated written 4 January 1797, inserted in files on 1 September 1797, Corr. Pol., vol. 48; "Objets qui doivent entrer dans la Negociation qui va souvir avec les États-Unis," 2 October 1797, ibid.; Alexandre Hauterive, "Plan à propose sur l'amérique," October 1797, ibid.; Pierre Adet to Talleyrand,

22 September 1797, ibid.; an untitled paper dated 21 October 1797, ibid. (hereafter, Plan of Negotiations.)
Another report, written by the previous foreign minister, Charles Delacroix, *Des Moyens de régéner la France* (Paris, 1797), was apparently not used by Talleyrand. Delacroix's only recommendation for reconciling the two countries was to propose the release of Lafayette, who was being held by the Austrian government. He was released in the fall of 1797. *Ibid.*, p. 303. The Otto memoir has been published, and all citations will be to the printed version. See Louis Otto, *Considérations sur la Conduite de Gouvernement Américain envers la France depuis le commencement de la Révolution jusqu'en 1797*, ed., Gilbert Chinard (Princeton, N.J., 1945), pp. 16-17, 26-27.

17. Durand Echeverria, *Mirage in the West* (Princeton, N.J., 1957), pp. 207-12, 222-23.

18. "Objets qui doivent," p. 282.

19. Plan of Negotiations, p. 315.

20. "Objets qui dovient," pp. 284, 285.

21. Ibid., p. 283; Plan of Negotiations, pp. 315-16; Hauterive, "Plan," p. 294.

22. "Objets qui doivent," pp. 281, 286; the Minister of Marine estimated that 222 American ships had been captured in the West Indies, Pléville le Pelley to Talleyrand, 21 October 1797, Corr. Pol., vol. 48.

23. Fauchet, *A Sketch*, p. 13; Plan of Negotiations, pp. 315-16; Objets qui doivent, p. 279; Otto, *Considérations*, p. 28.

24. Alexander DeConde, *Quasi-War* (New York, 1966), pp. 17-35.

25. Fauchet, *A Sketch*, p. 13; Plan of Negotiations, p. 311; Adet to Talleyrand, 22 September 1797, Corr. Pol., vol. 48.

26. Otto, *Considérations*, pp. 17-18, 23; Margaret O'Dwyer, "Louis Guillaume Otto in America," (Ph.D. diss., Northwestern University, 1954), pp. 21, 59.

27. Adet to Talleyrand, 22 September 1797, Corr. Pol., vol. 48.

28. Objets qui doivent, p. 278; Plan of Negotiations, pp. 314-15; Otto, *Considérations*, pp. 25-26.

29. Objets qui doivent, p. 283.

30. John Marshall Journal, 30 October and 8 November 1797, 4, 26 February 1798, Pickering Papers, Massachusetts Historical Society, Boston, Massachusetts (hereafter, Marshall Journal); John Marshall to Charles Lee, 3 November 1797, John Marshall Papers, Library of Congress, Washington, D.C.; Charles Pinckney to Henry DeSaussure, 4 November 1797, F 7, vol. 4269, Archives Nationales, Paris.

31. Plan of Negotiations, p. 311.

32. Hauterive, "Plan," pp. 294-95.

33. O'Dwyer, "Otto in America," p. 111. Joseph Fauchet had urged the acquisition of Louisiana in another memoir in 1795, but the second one, published in Philadelphia in 1797, makes no mention of Louisiana for obvious reasons. E. Wilson Lyon, "The Directory and the United States," *American Historical Review*, 43 (April 1938): 515. For the 1795 memoir, see Joseph Fauchet, "Mémoire sur les États-Unis d'Amerique," ed. Carl Lokke, American Historical Association, Annual Report for 1935 (Washington, 1938), 1: 85-119.

34. Hauterive, "Plan," pp. 294-95.

35. "Mémoire sur les relations entre la France et les Etats-Unis de 1792 à 1797," [8-14] October 1797, DeSages, vol. 36, Archives du Ministère des Affaires Étrangères, Paris. The memoir has been published and all references are to the printed edition. See William Stinchombe, ed., "A Neglected Memoir by Tallyrand on French-American Relations," American Philosophical Society, *Proceedings* 121 (June 1977): 195-208.

Tallyrand informed the American envoys on 8 October 1797, that he would finish the report in two or three days. Antoine-Eustache, Baron d'Osmond, first asked the Americans for an explanation of Adams's 16 May 1797 speech on 14 October 1797, indicating that the Directory had approved Talleyrand's report. See Marshall Journal, 8, 14 October 1797. The parts of Adams's speech which the French regarded as requiring explanation varied over the course of the envoys' stay, but four paragraphs were identified in which Adams charged the French with trying to separate the United States government from its people; his charge of French violations of the treaty of 1778; his recommendations of defensive measures because of "the Depredations of our Commerce"; and lastly, Adams's repetition of the charge that the French government sought to separate the American government from the people. See enclosure in American Envoys to Pickering, 22 October 1797, "Diplomatic Despatches, France," 6, Record Group 59, National Archives, Washington, D.C.

Other authors have cited a second Talleyrand memoir, [3-18] February 1798, Corr. Pol., vol. 49, but the first report explains in detail the policy that Talleyrand pursued from October to February. See Lyon, "The Directory and the United States," p. 522; DeConde, *Quasi-War*, (New York, 1966) pp. 44, 56-57; Marvin Zahniser, *Charles Cotesworth Pinckney*, (Chapel Hill, N.C., 1967), p. 179; Albert H. Bowman, *Struggle for Neutrality* (Knoxville, Tenn., 1974), pp. 312-16, 321. Bowman cites a document written on 2 October 1797 as another report approved by Talleyrand, but Talleyrand did not accept any of this report's recommendations on indemnities, cessation of hostilities, and the revision of treaties during the next nine months. Moreover, Talleyrand specifically rejected a number of the report's suggestions in his margin notes. The author of the premier French work on the Directory's foreign policy, Raymond Guyot, *Le Directoire et la Paix de l'Europe* (Paris: 1911), p. 34, missed the Talleyrand "Memoir on Relations between France and the United States," because he examined only Correspondance Politique, États-Unis, vols. 48, 49, for French-American relations in 1797-1798.

36. Palmer, *Age of the Democratic Revolution*, 2: 366.

37. Stinchcombe, ed., "Neglected Memoir," p. 206.

38. Ibid., p. 208.

39. Ibid., p. 204.

40. Ibid., p. 207.

41. Cf. Zahniser, *Pinckney*, pp. 166-68; DeConde, *Quasi-War*, pp. 46-48; Albert Beveridge, *The Life of John Marshall*, 4 vols. (Boston: 1916), 2: 247-50.

42. Marshall Journal, 14, 28 October 1797, 2 March 1798; American Envoys to Pickering, 8 November 1797 & 9 March 1798, "Diplomatic Despatches, France," 6 Record Group 59, Caron de Beaumarchais to American Envoys, 17 January 1798, Gerry Papers, Pierpont Morgan Library, New York, New York.

43. John Marshall to Charles Lee, 12 October 1797, "Diplomatic Despatches, France," 6, Record Group 59. (This letter was written over a period of almost three weeks with the last notes dated 27 October 1797.) Marshall Journal, 15, 18-[19] October 1797.

44. Talleyrand to American Envoys, 18 March 1798, Gerry Papers, Pierpont Morgan Library; American Envoys to Pickering, 9 March 1798, "Diplomatic Despatches, France," 6, Record Group 59.

45. Marshall Journal, 15 October 1797, American Envoys to Talleyrand, 3 April 1798, Corr. Pol., vol. 49.

46. American Envoys to Pickering, 8 November 1797, "Diplomatic Despatches, France," 6, Record Group 59.

47. Stinchcombe, ed., "Neglected Memoir," p. 199. All the following quotes are from ibid., pp. 201-207.

48. Ibid., p. 206.

4

"I Could a Tale Unfold"

In The Hague the Pinckney family took up residence at the Marshall Turenne tavern while they waited for word about Adams's policy toward France. Mary Pinckney showed signs of traveler's boredom, finding the Dutch weather more disagreeable than the French. "It is too cold even to walk at noon," she lamented to her cousin and companion of Parisian schooldays, Margaret Manigault. "For these ten days we have not seen the sun," she continued, and residents of The Hague had warned against walking along the seashore because the air there was "unwholesome."[1] Her husband Charles remained outwardly unperturbed by the long delay but grew increasingly impatient with the French and their policy. Every ship captured, every cargo condemned, every new affront to the United States was "rapidly rendering the name of 'Frenchmen' as hateful as it was once dear to Americans." Pinckney hoped that his countrymen were "all united in a determination to preserve their independence & in not submitting to a national disgrace."[2]

A delay in the preparation of his instructions had caused Marshall to wait in Philadelphia for more than two weeks, but on 18 June he departed on the brig *Grace* for Amsterdam. Traveling with him was his secretary, John Brown, a clerk of the general court in Richmond, and his friend Robert Gamble's eighteen-year-old son John, who was to make a tour of Europe under Marshall's watchful direction. According to Marshall's account, he had two Dutch shipmates, but evidently both were actually Frenchmen traveling under false passports.[3] Elbridge Gerry had intended to leave Boston soon after Marshall's departure on the ship *Union*, but bad weather delayed the embarkation until 9 August.[4]

As he awaited his colleagues' arrival, Pinckney obtained news of French policy from informants in Paris and from American travelers who had spent time there. James Mountflorence, an assistant to the American consul at Paris, Fulwar Skipwith, was his most frequent correspondent, and he also exchanged letters with James Pitcairn and Pierre S. DuPont de Nemours. George Izard, a cousin of Mary Pinckney's who was just completing his education outside Paris, visited the Pinckneys at The Hague as did relatives Charles Pinckney Horry and States Rutledge. When Thomas B. Adams, a son of the president, left Paris, he traveled to The Hague, where he talked to Pinckney and John Q. Adams, who was also awaiting reassignment. Thomas Adams related the new developments in Paris as explained to him in interviews with several members of the Directory. Louis and James Marshall, John's brothers, visited Paris on business in 1797, reporting their impressions to Pinckney and undoubtedly to their brother.[5]

Pinckney clearly analyzed the divisions within the French government and their implications for the United States. The moderates, as they were called by Americans, in the lower chamber had attacked the Directory's harsh policy toward the United States, and the Directory itself was badly divided on this issue. Jean Paul Ruebell, Paul Barras, and Louis-Marie La Revellière-Lépeaux advocated a continuation of the war on all fronts, while Lazare Carnot and François Barthélemy demanded that a more strenuous effort be made to reach an accommodation with Great Britain in the negotiations underway with Lord Malmesbury at Lille. Pinckney saw the third—and most unpredictable—consideration as the army's increasing involvement in French politics, a problem compounded by the rivalry between the army of Italy under Napoleon Bonaparte and the Army of the Sambre and Meuse under Louis Lazare Hoche. Pinckney wanted to get to Paris as quickly as possible, because he feared a shift of political alignments that would leave the moderates, and hence American interests, in a weakened position.[6]

Within days of Marshall's arrival at The Hague, the widely expected change in the French government occurred, in a coup on Dix-Huit Fructidor (4 September). A triumvirate within the Directory ordered the arrest of Directors Carnot and Barthélemy, canceled the results of the 1796 elections, closed more than thirty newspapers in Paris alone, and exiled critics in the Council of Five Hundred to French Guinea. They justified these actions as necessary to thwart a royalist reaction and preserve the republic. By its coup the ruling faction crushed the moderates and curtailed their influence on American policy for the immediate future.

Marshall and Pinckney predicted that the slim chances for peace had suffered permanent damage by the coup.[7] Marshall dismissed the "alleged conspiracy for the reestablishment of royalty," finding "not even a suspicion of its existence." To Washington he explained that "Necessity the never to be worn out apology for violence, is alleged," but "it is a truth that requires no demonstration that if a republican form of government cannot be administered by the general will, it cannot be administered against that will by an army." The gulf between the envoys' conception of government and the character of the Directory and the revolution could not have been greater. Referring to the "law of 'Public Safety'," Pinckney noted that it was "said by some to be enacted to preserve and support the existing Constitution." But, he noted, "By referring to the Constitution, you will be able to appreciate this assertion without any comment."[8]

Even before the coup, however, a majority of the Directory had opposed acknowledging the Jay Treaty and sought an apology from the United States for compromising with Great Britain. The victorious directors showed the open hostility to the United States that Pinckney had feared. The deposed Carnot was equally antagonistic, urging French expansion into Louisiana and Florida. By way of warning to other neutrals, he suggested that the free city of Hamburg pay France to preserve its neutrality.[9] To the envoys of the Cisalpine Republic, La Revellière-Lépeaux publicly proclaimed in August 1797, "The Directory will not treat with the Enemies of the Republic."[10] Reubell insisted that President Adams had insulted France and betrayed the French by supporting Jay's Treaty, further maintaining that peace with the United States would be impossible as long as Adams served as president.[11] Negotiation, much less peace, between the two countries would be difficult.

Pinckney and Marshall decided to give Gerry until 18 September, then they would set out for Paris alone. Pinckney explained to

Pickering that "some hints I have received from Paris suggest the propriety of our hastening to that city at this juncture." Actually, the two envoys had determined earlier to leave without Gerry if necessary. [12] En route to Paris they learned that Gerry had landed on the day they left, and they slowed their pace in hopes that the third envoy would catch up with them. Instead of rushing on to Paris, however, Gerry visited Amsterdam and departed the Netherlands almost a week later. He wrote ahead to request that Mary Pinckney hire a valet for him, making his arrival in Paris a week after his colleagues, on 4 October. [13]

James Mountflorence had rented a house for the entire American delegation at 1131 Rue Grenelle, in what is now the seventh arrondissement, an address that was only three blocks from the foreign ministry on Rue de Bac. On the fourth floor lived the owner of the house. The third floor accommodated the three secretaries, John Brown, Henry Rutledge, who was Pinckney's nephew, and Bossenger Foster, Jr., a Bostonian in Europe on business for Andrew Craigie, who had recommended him to Gerry. The Pinckneys and their eleven-year-old daughter Mary occupied the main floor, and Gerry and Marshall had a small ground-floor apartment that opened onto a courtyard. Gerry complained that his quarters were so dangerous that he had to keep two pistols under his pillow. Mary Pinckney described the furnishings as "not very fresh" and the mirrors as cracked. The provisions for the Americans were "sparingly sound in sheets but no towels." The rent, payable in advance, was exorbitant, and the entire mission lived together in close quarters. [14]

After Gerry's arrival, the envoys immediately asked to call upon Talleyrand. He received them two days later, and in contrast to the treatment given Pinckney earlier in the year, offered the cards of hospitality necessary to protect the envoys against deportation. These were delivered by the police the next morning. During their fifteen-minute conversation Talleyrand asked the envoys to postpone their request to begin negotiations until he finished his report on French-American relations, which needed the Directory's approval. [15] The Americans willingly obliged the master of procrastination.

The envoys had heard nothing for over a week when Baron d'Osmond, one of Talleyrand's private secretaries, told Mountflorence that the Directory expected an explanation of certain offensive parts of Adams's speech at the opening of the special session of Congress on 16 May. D'Osmond indicated that the statement of explanation by the envoys would have to be given before the Directory would consider receiving them officially. The envoys decided to make no response to this overture, since, as they argued to themselves, the information came to them only indirectly. [16] They also decided, a critical decision, to offer no explanation of the president's speech, because to do so would indicate an insult to the president and to American sovereignty. This decision remained unaltered during the next six months, despite repeated indications from the French, including Talleyrand directly, that some kind of explanation would be necessary if the envoys were to be officially received. [17]

Contrary to the advice of two of the most knowledgeable Americans in Paris, the envoys decided to press ahead for negotiations without official recognition. Leading the American community in Paris was Joel Barlow, whose actions belied his claim that "ever since the year 1793 when I came near to perishing with the fathers of the Republic, because they were my friends, I have avoided any connections with men in power." Barlow could not resist meddling in French-American affairs, and after the first approach to the envoys, he noted that Talleyrand "gave our Ministers several indirect hints not to press any thing but to have patience." Fulwar Skipwith agreed with Barlow's expectations concerning the speed of the negotiations, but his advice was ignored. [18]

Three days after d'Osmond's approach, Nicholas Hubbard, identified as W in the envoys' published dispatches, called on Pinckney to request that he accept a visit from Jean Conrad Hottinguer, X of WXYZ. [19] Hubbard was an Englishman by birth and a junior partner in the Amsterdam banking firm of Van Staphorst and Hubbard, which was the American government's European bank. He assured Pinckney that Hottinguer was a man of honor, an explanation that Pinckney accepted without seeking more detail. On the evening of 18 October, Hottinguer informed Pinckney that

Figure 2. Joel Barlow by Robert Fulton, 1805. *Courtesy of the Indianapolis Museum of Art. Gift of Mr. and Mrs. Eli Lilly.*

the American government was expected to assume all of the claims of American citizens against the French government, pay an indemnity to American merchantmen for French confiscations, grant a loan to the French government of 32 million Dutch guilders, and provide an additional *pot de vin*, or bribe, of fifty thousand pounds to Talleyrand.[20]

When Pinckney informed his amazed colleagues, they jointly requested that Hottinguer present the proposal to all the envoys. Without realizing it, the Americans had allowed the opening of informal negotiations with unofficial French agents, and these discussions were to continue throughout the envoys' stay in Paris despite their avowed determination not to conduct such negotiations. Hottingeur outlined the proposal to the three envoys, mentioning that he made his request in the name of a man close to Talleyrand. Faced with an abrupt American refusal, Hottinguer introduced this man—Pierre Bellamy, Y of WXYZ—at a meeting the next day, when they elaborated on the proposals.[21] In the first days of negotiations with Hottinguer and Bellamy the inexperienced envoys were aghast at their situation; they would agree only to send one of their number back to the United States for more instructions, provided the French government ceased attacks on American shipping during the interim. Having broken off peace talks with Great Britain during the week, the French refused the condition.[22]

Responding to the Americans' resolute stand, Talleyrand sent an emissary to call upon Gerry. He was Lucien Hauteval, Z of WXYZ, a wealthy West Indian sugar planter. Forced to flee Santo Domingo in 1792, Hauteval had moved to Boston, where he met Gerry. By 1796 he was in Paris, scheming to be named French minister to the United States. Hauteval assured Gerry that Talleyrand deeply desired peace and would welcome more private contacts with the envoys.[23] From this time forward, Hauteval's role in the negotiations would be to proclaim Talleyrand's sincerity whenever the talks seemed to be breaking down. On this occasion he explained that a loan to France and a bribe to Talleyrand were necessary. But he also wanted it understood that he did not come as a representative bearing Talleyrand's proposals as had Hottinguer and Bellamy. Talleyrand distinguished between those who approached the Americans to keep the negotiations open and those associates whom he trusted to negotiate in his name. Although Hauteval was devoted to French-American peace and sought to influence Talleyrand, he served only as a high-level errand boy without responsibility in the negotiations.[24]

A week passed after Hauteval's visit before Hottinguer and Bellamy reappeared. Probably this timing was related to the signing of the triumphant settlement with Austria at Campo Formio. French demands now became tougher and more threatening. The United States would suffer the same fate as Venice, which France had awarded to Austria. Under the genius of Napoleon, France would soon launch an attack on Great Britain; then the United States would have to face French displeasure alone. Hottinguer and Bellamy suggested that if Madison or Burr had been sent, a settlement would have been reached; they threatened to provoke civil war in the United States by encouraging the partisans of France against the Federalists. Before this blustering the envoys held firm, rejecting all claims, although they did accept a copy of the parts of Adams's speech that had offended the Directory. At this time Pinckney made his well-known response to Hottinguer's insistence on a bribe: "No, No, not a sixpence."[25]

The first phase of the negotiations ended, and it was the record of these meetings that was published in April 1798 for the American public to read. Privately in Paris both sides showed frustration over the initial results. Gerry wrote, "The fact is, as I conceive it, that a small cargo of Mexican dollars would be more efficient in a negotiation at present than two Cargoes of Ambassadors." Pinckney took a sterner view, placing the emphasis on national honor, a standard he maintained more earnestly than the other two envoys in the following months. "We experience a haughtiness which is unexampled in the history and practice of nations," he wrote to William Vans Murray, "and feel ourselves under the necessity of submitting to circumstances which make an impression to be worn out, you may be assured, only with life. I would give a handsome fee for one half hour with you. I could a tale unfold."[26]

The impasse in the negotiations caused the resourceful Talleyrand to change his agents if not his tactics. Historians have given undue emphasis to the infrequent meetings held between the envoys and Hottinguer and Bellamy after November; they have failed to note the new intermediaries who kindled the envoys' hopes and kept them in Paris for five more months. This second group of intermediaries, including Louis d'Autremont, Caron de Beaumarchais,

Joseph Pitcairn, and Pierre du Pont to Nemours—to name several of the more important examples—now maintained contacts between Talleyrand and the envoys. In the last months of the mission these new agents conducted the negotiations under the close supervision of Bellamy and Talleyrand.

Despite the American rebuff, the French continued to apply pressure. Hauteval called on Gerry to ask if the envoys had informed other ministers of the bribe demands. Gerry informed him that the subject was considered confidential; he added, however, that he would not meet with Hauteval again, since Hauteval had no authority to negotiate. The French also approached James Mountflorence, through whom they had made their first overture to the envoys; Pinckney shut off that avenue of access. Acting on Talleyrand's instructions, Pitcairn called on Marshall and Pinckney to determine it they were ready to reconsider the loan question. Pinckney ruefully mentioned that the idea had been discussed but explained that because it was against their instructions, the envoys would not consider it. [27]

Talleyrand now entered the picture directly for the first time, taking the occasion of a dinner party to express his displeasure with the envoys. Speaking to John Trumbull, he remarked that the envoys were three thousand miles from home and should take it upon themselves to reach the right decision to preserve peace without waiting for new instructions. The Americans, moreover, should realize that the "French were impatient" and that the problem required a quick solution, which meant acceding to the bribe and loan demands. [28]

Still resolute, the envoys attempted no appraisal of the situation in Paris. They viewed French interests and conduct almost as if the French Revolution had not occurred. Their interpretation of Talleyrand's tactics focused only on the foreign minister's corruption. The envoys failed to analyze the group of agents and secretaries whom Talleyrand had chosen to confer with them. Rumors of bribes were rampant in Paris. During the seven months the envoys spent there, Talleyrand accepted bribes channeled through intermediaries, particularly Bellamy, from Portugal and Great Britain. Sandoz Rollin heard that Spain had contributed a vast sum and suggested that Prussia do likewise for self-protection.[29] Nicholas Hubbard and Wilhelm Willink, another Dutch banker, told the envoys that bribery was indispensable in Paris.[30] Even though they would have no guarantee of success, to do business with the French government at this time, the Americans would have to offer a bribe or otherwise play the dangerous game of outwaiting Talleyrand. He and his associates had in fact turned the Ministry of Foreign Affairs into a house of commerce. Talleyrand's partners, Hottinguer, Bellamy, and Hubbard, sought to use the foreign minister's position to enhance their private speculations.

We can better understand the insistence on the bribe and loan demands if we examine the economic interests linking Hottinguer, Bellamy, Hubbard, and Talleyrand. Neither Bellamy nor Hottinguer concealed his land investments in the United States from the envoys.[31] Hubbard, moreover, was not simply a partner in Van Staphorst and Hubbard, the firm that had financed the American national debt. He was also a member of an openly acknowledged Dutch banking syndicate that speculated in land and currency in the United States.[32] Hottinguer had met Pinckney before in Amsterdam, if not in Charleston. John Marshall knew that his own brother James had negotiated a loan through Hottinguer the previous summer in Amsterdam.[33] Of the four, Bellamy was perhaps the least known to Americans, although Pitcairn and Rufus King were acquainted with him.[34]

The activities of Talleyrand's three partners reveal the instability of French society in 1797. These men were temporarily set adrift by the French Revolution and were seeking new outlets for investment that would be safe from the vicissitudes of European wars. Jean Conrad Hottinguer was a former Zurich banker who had come to Paris in the 1780s as a representative of Swiss banking interests. He established his own bank in Paris but was forced to leave in 1793, and he fled to London to avoid imprisonment and probable death. While in London he married an American, Elizabeth Redwood of Newport, Rhode Island.[35] Hottinguer directed a group of German emigrants settling in Georgia in 1794 on behalf of a company, the Georgia Agricultural Company, of which he was part owner.[36] By mid-1795, Hottinguer moved to Philadelphia, conducting business with Talleyrand and with the head of the Holland Land Company in America, Theophile Cazenove.[37]

Cazenove had worked with Talleyrand in Paris in the 1780s. He advised Talleyrand on American speculations and employed him to write reports on prospects for buying land in Maine and New York. Later Cazenove lived with Talleyrand in Paris as a financial adviser, much to the disgust of Cazenove's sister.[38]

Hottinguer joined a consortium with Cazenove and Talleyrand to buy land in Pennsylvania, certainly from Robert Morris and his son-in-law James Marshall, and probably from others.[39] In 1796 Hottinguer returned to London and went on to Hamburg, where he formed a new land company to sell American property to émigrés. He named Pierre Bellamy as secretary of the new company, and the banking firm of Bellamy and Ricci invested in the scheme.[40] After a visit to Amsterdam, Hottinguer returned to Paris to raise money for the new company. In 1798 he opened his own bank in Paris, giving special attention to American affairs and Talleyrand's far-flung financial dealings.[41] Hottinguer and Talleyrand were to remain close associates for the next three decades. Of the WXYZ agents he and Hubbard were not publicly identified in the scandals following collapse of the American negotiations.

Like Hottinguer, Talleyrand had returned to England after a period of exile. He had first arranged through Danton to obtain an unofficial mission to London; he was later declared an émigré by the National Convention, thus making it unsafe for him to return to France. Talleyrand remained in England until the Pitt government passed a new alien law designed to expel obnoxious Frenchmen. He then took refuge in Philadelphia in 1794. After having his name removed from the émigré list, Talleyrand departed the United States in the spring of 1796. He left his papers in the hands of Cazenove, some land in Cazenove's name, and sizable investments in United States bank stock in the name of James Cazenove, a nephew of Theophile.[42] Returning to Europe, Talleyrand was met in Hamburg by Gabriel-Marie, Comte de Ricci, a French émigré and Bellamy's partner.[43] Talleyrand then traveled to Amsterdam, where he conducted business with his associate Hubbard on their American investments.[44] Probably not coincidentally,

Talleyrand and Hottinguer returned from Amsterdam to Paris on the same day to continue their business ventures.[45] James Pitcairn reported that Talleyrand arrived back in Paris with "budgets of financial schemes."[46]

Educated as a clergyman, Pierre Bellamy tutored and then married a banker's daughter, soon finding his true calling in banking. Because of the influence of his father-in-law, Bellamy rose rapidly in the Geneva government, becoming a member of the Council of Two Hundred in 1791 and then auditor the next year. In the revolution of 1794 he was imprisoned under charges of counter-revolutionary activities. Expecting to receive a death sentence, Bellamy saved his life by a brilliant speech before the tribunal; he was sentenced instead to permanent exile. Moving to Hamburg wth his wife and four children, Bellamy established a new bank with Ricci, combining his banking activities with those of an import merchant. He was reputed to have a haughty, offensive personality, an impression borne out in his meetings with the American envoys.[47]

Another figure who became crucial in the American negotiations could be included in this group—Caron de Beaumarchais. Exiled from France in 1792, he took up residence in Hamburg, returning to Paris just after Talleyrand and Hottinguer. Beaumarchais was an investor in the ill-fated Scioto Company on the Ohio River and later with Pierre S. DuPont and Talleyrand in the purchase of Kentucky lands.[48] In late 1796, Talleyrand became Beaumarchais's financial adviser, recommending that he conduct his importing business through Bellamy and Ricci. Beaumarchais appointed Theophile Cazenove as his head agent in the United States, and, again on Talleyrand's recommendation, he hired Alexander Hamilton as his lawyer to handle claims against the American government.[49] Beaumarchais boasted that Talleyrand had promised to use his position as foreign minister to secure payment of his American claims.[50]

This group had several distinctive characteristics. Excluding Hauteval, all had been connected with banking in Paris before the revolution. None was politically prominent, but all had faced almost certain death if they remained in Paris, St. Marc, or Geneva. All had cooperated with their respective governments in the early stages of revolution and then fled. Hottinguer had married an American, and it was reported that Hauteval had married an un-identified "Boston Lady" during his residence in that city.[51] They all kept their funds sequestered in neutral Hamburg, which was a convenient port for trade with the United States at this time.

These men also had heavy financial interests in American lands and stocks. All of them thus had a vested interest in maintaining peace with the United States. As often happened in eighteenth-century diplomacy, the line between public service and personal interests became blurred.[52] The WXY (Hubbard, Hottinguer, Bellamy) affair, as it might be called in view of Hauteval's minor role, resulted from the machinations of a small, interconnected group of recently returned exiles working with Talleyrand to re-build their fortunes while secondarily preserving peace. Because their interests had no connection with privateering but could only be harmed by it, these men were more willing than others in the French government to limit maritime abuses. For all the public outcry in the United States when the dispatches were published, the agents whose actions seemed so nefarious were more inclined to prevent war with the United States than were the members of the Directory. In delaying negotiations, Talleyrand and his associates did not intend to risk the peace but to reward themselves.

The American delegation itself was divided on the importance of remaining in Paris. From the time of his appointment Gerry be-lieved that the best strategy was to prolong the talks as much as possible, since this tactic, he believed, would prevent war. French policymakers would finally come to the realization that war with the United States would greatly strengthen the British war effort against France. This attitude explains, in part, his receptivity to Talleyrand's delaying tactics. Total failure of the mission, Gerry wrote, would bring war and, more important, "disgrace republicanism and make it the scoff of despots."[53] Pinckney quickly grew disenchanted with Gerry, complaining that his colleague was "habitually suspicious, and hesitates so much, that it is very unpleasant to do business with him." Pinckney further noted French attempts to divide the envoys and observed that "Some civilities are shewn to Mr G[erry] and none to the two others."[54]

Figure 3. Charles C. Pinckney by John Trumbull, 1791. *Courtesy of the Yale University Art Gallery.*

Marshall, too, became increasingly restive and sought to force the French to negotiate or suspend the mission, a reaction that

Alexandre Hauterive, a confidant of Talleyrand, had predicted before the negotiations began.[55] Marshall did not expect war if the negotiations failed, and this was the basis of his disagreement with Gerry. Three months in Paris had strengthened his conviction that France was not a republic.[56]

The difference among the envoys became apparent to the French by mid-December, when Bellamy and Hottinguer intervened directly for the last time. Hottinguer called on Pinckney under the pretense of seeking advice on his Georgia landholdings. But Hottinguer's main interest was to determine if the envoys were willing to consider a loan. Meeting as a group for the first time in almost a month, the envoys reiterated their position and added that they would treat only with officially accredited agents. A few days later a woman, probably Madame de la Forest, told Pinckney at a dinner party that the Americans must offer a loan or they would not be received.[57] Under pressure from Rufus King either to begin negotiations or to leave Paris, the envoys drew up a memorial listing American grievances. They originally intended to request their passports, but Gerry refused to take such a step, thus allowing the informal negotiations to continue.[58]

Bellamy now approached Marshall, undoubtedly in conjunction with Hottinguer's visit to Pinckney, to inquire whether Marshall would consider agreeing to pay Beaumarchais's claim against Virginia as the personal bribe to Talleyrand, a step that would allow the negotiations to begin again. Bellamy explained that the Beaumarchais claim could be included in the final peace settlement with the United States accepting responsibility for its payment. The new bribe proposal would allow Talleyrand and his associates immediate access to needed capital. Beaumarchais had urged Bellamy to present this proposal in just such a context.[59]

Marshall replied equivocally that he would consider the proposal but only if Americans' claims against the French government were also included in the final settlement, a proposition that, if accepted, would have appreciably advanced the negotiations. Bellamy made no answer to Marshall's proposal, however. When Marshall informed Pinckney of his talk with Bellamy, he said that he would not commit himself on the question, since he was Beaumarchais's lawyer for claims against the state of Virginia. Pinckney rejected

Bellamy's proposition out of hand, correctly seeing it as another bribe request. After the publication of the dispatches in Europe in 1798, Bellamy complained to Beaumarchais that it had been a simple proposition bearing no implications of corruption. To Joseph Pitcairn, who had moved to Hamburg, Bellamy gave another explanation, saying that he wanted to get the "£100,000 throu[gh] his hands." Bellamy had conceived the idea "from having heard that Marshall's brother had bought one similarly situated for 50 p[er]cent."[60] Bellamy's allusion was to John and James Marshall's purchase of the Fairfax claims in northern Virginia during James's negotiations with Hottinguer in Amsterdam.[61]

On the day before Christmas the Directory ordered Talleyrand to seek loans from the envoys of the free city of Hamburg and the United States. Talleyrand was to request that each group agree to buy Dutch bonds at par.[62] Since the Dutch issues were selling at less that 50 percent of par, this would represent a grant to the French government. Eventually Hamburg did subscribe to the loan in a futile effort to prevent a French takeover, but the American envoys refused. Not by coincidence, the new policy brought profit to Hubbard, Bellamy, and Hottinguer, and to their banking partners in Amsterdam and Hamburg as well.

Talleyrand decided to interpret the Directory's new instructions in a complicated fashion. Marshall's response, as contrasted with Pinckney's blunt refusal to Bellamy and Hottinguer, dictated Talleyrand's next move. It had long been assumed that Talleyrand selected Gerry as the most amenable envoy, as charged by Pinckney, and sought to deal with him alone. In reality, Talleyrand intended to exclude Pinckney alone and continue negotiations with Marshall and Gerry. Scholars have accepted Marshall's own account of the negotiations in his Journal, in which he depicted himself and Pinckney as equally adamant against the French. Actually, they were not. Nor can the division within the commission be attributed to Gerry alone. Marshall accepted and participated in the virtual exclusion of Pinckney from January until March.

A shift in lodging by Gerry and Marshall in the middle of November had facilitated Pinckney's later exclusion. The two envoys' new landlady was Madame de Villette, described by Voltaire as "Belle et Bonne." Voltaire had arranged for her marriage in 1777 to the Marquis de Villette, whose behavior before and after marriage can be best described by the Victorian definition of degenerate. During Voltaire's last visit to Paris in 1778 he stayed with Madame and the Marquis de Villette, and after his death the one bond sustaining the marriage was mutual worship of Voltaire. Following her husband's death in 1793, Madame de Villette was incarcerated for royalist leanings for ten months. Short of funds, she moved in 1796 to 54 Rue de Vaugirard, near the residence of Joel Barlow, who probably recommended her house to Gerry.[63]

Figure 4.   Madame de Villette and Voltaire (Charles) de Villette by John Vanderlyn. *Courtesy of Senate House Historic Site, Palisades Interstate Park Commission, New York State Office of Parks and Recreation.*

The new apartments had some peculiarities, but Marshall and Gerry did not mention them. A robe belonging to Voltaire occupied a prominent place, as did a few of his letters. The drawing room's central attraction was a marble bust of Voltaire, under which Madame de Villette burned incense. After some legal conflicts, she had also obtained Voltaire's heart, which was preserved in a glass jar in the drawing room. After a glowing description of Madame de Villette to his wife, Gerry added almost by way of an afterthought, "I have given you a particular history of this lady, without her suspicion that I have any information relating to her, & of my present situation, knowing it will gratify you to hear how minutely I am situated."[64] In their new setting Madame de Villette offered her American tenants social services not often found in revolutionary Paris. She accompanied Marshall to the theater—for a Voltaire play, of course; she went with both envoys to the opera; she taught Gerry French; she sat with them each afternoon for hours; and she organized parties and dinners for her American friends.[65]

Madame de Villette's role in the negotiations has long intrigued scholars. In two recent accounts of the XYZ affair she is described as Talleyrand's agent.[66] However titillating it would be to have a *femme fatale* influencing the course of negotiations, there is simply no evidence that Madame de Villette was Talleyrand's agent. The Paris police did have an informer who watched Madame de Villette's house for visitors. Posing as a wine merchant, this police agent, known as Kahion, regularly entered her house, but he was unable to steal any papers.[67]

At Madame de Villette's house Talleyrand pursued his new strategy of isolating Pinckney. Gerry had invited a number of Frenchmen, including Hottinguer, Bellamy, Hauteval, and Beaumarchais, as well as American residents in Paris, to a dinner party. There Talleyrand's agents asked Gerry for a bribe—the last time it was mentioned—and a loan. Gerry angrily refused both requests. Talleyrand, who rarely did his own dirty work, had one of his aides inform Gerry that the government would no longer negotiate with Pinckney.[68]

After three months in Paris, the envoys were still not officially received. Demands for loans and bribes were continuing. In his determined effort to divide the American envoys, Talleyrand turned to Americans in Paris to apply pressure to the envoys, particularly Gerry, to reach a settlement. In January and February the three envoys rarely met, and most of the informal negotiations were conducted by other Americans, so it is important to examine this group in detail to see how they attempted to influence the negotiations.

Notes

1. Mary Pinckney to Margaret Manigault, 11 June 1797, Manigault Family Papers, University of South Carolina, Columbia, South Carolina.

2. Charles Pinckney to Joseph Pitcairn, 6 April, 20 July 1797, Pitcairn Papers, Cincinnati Historical Society, Cincinnati, Ohio.

3. John Marshall to Mary Marshall, 20 July 1797, Marshall Papers, College of William and Mary, Williamsburg, Virginia; Joseph Létombe to Talleyrand, 24 July 1797, Correspondance Politique, États-Unis, vol. 48, Archives du Ministère des Affairs Étrangères, Paris (hereafter, Corr. Pol.).

4. Elbridge Gerry to Charles C. Pinckney, 20 September 1797 in *Elbridge Gerry's Letterbook: Paris, 1797-1798*, ed. Russell W. Knight (Salem, 1966), pp. 7-8.

5. Mary Pinckney to Margaret Manigault, 11 June and 8 September 1797, Manigault Family Papers; John Q. Adams Diary, 2, 8, 11 June 1797, Adams Papers, Massachusetts Historical Society, Boston, Massachusetts; Charlotte Murray to Eliza Wolcott, 14 June 1797, Oliver Wolcott Papers, vol. 54, Connecticut Historical Society, Hartford, Connecticut.

6. Charles Pinckney to Elbridge Gerry, 23 August 1797, Gerry Letterbook, Gerry Papers, Library of Congress, Washington, D.C.; Pinckney to Timothy Pickering, [14] September 1797 (misdated 24 September 1797), "Diplomatic Despatches, France," 5, Record Group 59, Washington, D.C.; for the politics within the Directory and peace negotiations, see Marcel Reinhard, "Les Négociations de Lille et la Crise du 18 Fructidor d'après la Correspondance inédite de Colchen," *Revue d'Histoire Moderne et Contemporaine* 5 (1958): 44, 45, 49.

7. Charles Pinckney to Timothy Pickering, [14] September 1797, "Diplomatic Despatches, France," 5, Record Group 59.

8. Quotes from John Marshall to Timothy Pickering, 15 September 1797, "Diplomatic Despatches, France," 6, Record Group 59, Marshall to George Washington, 15 September 1797, Washington Papers, Library of Congress, Washington, D.C.; Pinckney to Timothy Pickering, [14] September 1797, "Diplomatic Despatches, France," 5, Record Group 59.

9. Marcel Reinhard, *Le Grand Carnot*, 2 vols. (Paris: 1962), 2: 374 n10, 375 n15; Sandoz Rollin dispatch, 6 May 1796, in *Preussen und Frankreich von 1795 bis 1807: Diplomatische Correspondenzen*, 2 vols., ed. Paul Bailleu (Leipzig, 1881-1887), 1: 67 (hereafter, *Dip. Corr.*).

10. George LeFebvre, *The Thermidorians and the Directory*, trans. Robert Baldick (New York, 1964), p. 334, Georgia Robison, *Revellière-Lépeaux, Citizen Director* (New York, 1938), p. 218.

11. Bernard Narbonne, *Le Diplomatie du Directorie et Bonaparte d'après les inédites de Reubell* (Paris, 1951), pp. 85-86, 172-73; Gerlof Homan, "The Revolutionary Career of Jean François Reubell," (Ph.D. diss., University of Kansas, 1958), pp. 347-48.

12. Pinckney to Timothy Pickering, [14] September 1797, "Diplomatic Despatches, France," 5, Record Group 59; Mary Pinckney to Margaret Manigault, 8 September 1797, Manigault Family Papers; Marshall to Timothy Pickering, 15 September 1797, "Diplomatic Despatches, France," 6, Record Group 59.

13. Marshall to Charles Lee, 22 September 1797, Emmet Collection, New York Public Library, New York, New York; Charles Pinckney to Elbridge Gerry, 25 September 1797, Autograph Letters, Houghton Library, Harvard University, Cambridge, Massachusetts; Henry Rutledge to Edward Rutledge, 2 October 1797, Dreer Collection, Historical Society of Pennsylvania, Philadelphia, Pennsylvania.

14. Ibid.; quotes are from Mary Pinckney to Margaret Manigault, 5 October 1797, Manigault Family Papers; Elbridge Gerry to Ann Gerry, 25 November 1797, Gerry Papers; American Envoys to Talleyrand, 6 October 1797, Corr. Pol., vol. 48.

15. William Stinchcombe, ed., "A Neglected Memoir of Talleyrand on French-American Relations," American Philosophical Society *Proceedings* 121 (1977), pp. 195-98; William Stinchcombe, "Talleyrand and the American Negotiations of 1797-1798," *Journal of American History* 62 (1975): 276-83.

16. American Envoys to Timothy Pickering, 22 October 1797, "Diplomatic Despatches, France," 6, Record Group 59.; Marshall Journal, 14 October 1797 in the Pickering Papers, Massachusetts Historical Society, Boston, Massachusetts; for the identification of d'Osmond, see William Stinchcombe, "The Diplomacy of the WXYZ Affair," *William and Mary Quarterly* 34 (1977): 597.

17. Marshall Journal, 14 October 1797; Caron de Beaumarchais to Gerry and Marshall, 17 January 1798, Gerry Papers, Pierpont Morgan Library, New York, New York; American Envoys to Timothy Pickering, 9 March 1798, "Diplomatic Despatches, France," 6, Record Group 59.

18. Quotes are from Joel Barlow to James Cathalan, 14 June 1799, 29 October 1797, Joel Barlow Papers, vol. 4, Harvard University, Cambridge, Massachusetts; Fulwar Skipwith to James Monroe, 20 October 1797, Monroe Papers, Library of Congress, Washington, D.C.

19. W was Nicholas Hubbard; X was Jean Conrad Hottinguer; Y was Pierre Bellamy; and Z was Lucien Hauteval. There has been some confusion as to the identification of Hubbard as W, but in the Marshall Journal, 30 October 1797 and in American Envoys to Timothy Pickering, 22 October 1797, "Diplomatic Despatches, France," 6, Record Group 59, Hubbard is named, and there is no doubt that he is W. In a note inserted in the Adams Papers, 22 October 1797, the date of the envoys' dispatch, Adams wrote W over Hubbard's name. William Vans Murray, Commonplace Book, II, 13 June 1798, Murray Papers, Library of Congress, Washington, D.C., also identifies Hubbard as W. But Alexander DeConde, *The Quasi-War* (New York, 1966), p. 72, identified Caron Beaumarchais as W, an error repeated by Albert H. Bowman, *The Struggle for Neutrality* (Knoxville, 1974), p. 317n; Albert Beveridge, *The Life of John Marshall*, 4 vols. (Boston, 1916-1919), 2: 259, states that W was a Paris businessman.

The identification of the agents by French scholars is more confusing and lacks documentation. L. G. Michaud, ed., *Biographie Universelle* 85 vols. (Paris, 1811-1862), 83: 201, 203, names Bellamy as X and adds that the approach of Pinckney was made by three intimates of Talleyrand, Casimir de Montrond, André d'Arbelles, and Pierre Sainte-Foy. This mistaken identification is continued by Raymond Guyot, *Les Directorie et la Paix l'Europe* (Paris, 1911), pp. 561-62; and Georges LaCour-Gayet, *Talleyrand*, 4 vols. (Paris, 1930-1933), 1: 238. Bernard Fay, *L'Espirit révolutionnaire en France et États-Unis à la fin du XVIIIe Siècle* (Paris, 1925), p. 405, utilizes American sources but mentions only Bellamy and Hauteval as agents. Henri Malo, however, in *Le Beau Montrond* (Paris, 1926) combines the two traditions by naming Hottinguer, Bellamy, and Hauteval as the official agents and identifying Montrond, Sainte-Foy, and d'Arbelles as the unofficial agents.

We also have some knowledge of the later activities of the agents. Sometime in the Napoleonic era, Hubbard moved to Paris. Pieter Van Winter, *Het Aandeel van de Amsterdamschen handel ann den opbouw van het Amerikannasche Gemeenebest*, 2 vols. (The Hague, 1927-1933), 1: 200, 2: 282-83; Nicholas Hubbard to J. Van Beech Vollenhoven, 13 November 1812, Brants Archives, 206 Gemeentearchief, Amsterdam. John Conrad Hottinguer became a regent of the Bank of France and was created a baron by Napoleon. Romauld Szramkiewicz, *Les Régents et Censeurs de la Banque nommés sous le Consulat et l'Empire* (Geneva,

1974), pp. 168-76; Herbert Lüthy, *La Banque Protestante en France*, 2 vols. (Paris, 1961), 2: 544, 722-26.

20. American Envoys to Timothy Pickering, 22 October 1797; "Diplomatic Despatches, France," 6, Record Group 59, Marshall Journal, 18-[19] October 1797.

21. For the background information on Bellamy, see John Q. Adams to Rufus King, 11 July 1798, Adams Papers; Jacques Galiffe, *Notices Généalogiques sur les Familles Genevoises* 3 vols. (Geneva, 1836), 3: 43; for Bellamy's public explanation of his services to Talleyrand, see his statement, 25 June 1798, Corr. Pol., États-Unis, Supplement, 2.

22. Marshall to Charles Lee, October 12-[27], "Diplomatic Despatches, France," 6, Record Group 59; American Envoys to Timothy Pickering, 22 October 1797, ibid.

23. American Envoys to Timothy Pickering, 8 November 1797, ibid.; for the background on Hauteval and his American connections, see John Q. Adams to William V. Murray, 17 July 1798, Adams Papers; William Lee Diary, 20 March 1796, Lee-Palfrey Papers, vol. 2, Library of Congress, Washington, D.C.; Gabriel Debien, *Études Antillaises* (Paris, 1956), p. 156, 156n; Carl Seaburg and Stanley Paterson, *Merchant Prince of Boston* (Cambridge, 1971), pp. 77-79; 8, 23, 24 November, 17 December 1792, Nathaniel Cutting Journal, Massachusetts Historical Society, Boston, Mass.

24. Talleyrand to the Directory, 1 June 1798, Corr. Pol., vol. 49; Marshall to Timothy Pickering, 28 September 1798, Adams Papers; Lucien Hauteval to John Adams, 26 August 1798, ibid.

25. American Envoys to Timothy Pickering, 8 November 1798, "Diplomatic Despatches, France," 6, Record Group 59.

26. Gerry to William V. Murray, 30 October 1797; Pinckney to Murray, 30 October 1797, both enclosed in Murray to Timothy Pickering, 10 November 1797, "Diplomatic Despatches, The Netherlands," 3, Record Group 59, National Archives, Washington, D.C.

27. Hauteval to Elbridge Gerry, 4 November 1797, Gerry Papers, Pierpont Morgan Library; Pinckney to James Mountflorence, 7 November 1797, Knight-Gerry Papers, Massachusetts Historical Society, Boston, Massachusetts; Marshall Journal, [22-28] November 1797.

28. Note book, November 1797, King Papers, vol. 73, New-York Historical Society, New York.

29. Sandoz Rollin dispatches, 21 January and 28 March 1798, *Dip. Corr.*, 1: 168, 182; Guyot, *Le Directorie*, pp. 444, 446n, 469; Lüthy, *La Banque Protestante*, 2: 662; for other accounts, see Rufus King to American Envoys, 24 November 1797, King Papers, vol. 32, New-York Histori-

cal Society; King to American Envoys, 24 December 1797, King Papers, Library of Congress, Washington, D.C.; John Trumbull to Elbridge Gerry [January 1798], Trumbull Papers, Library of Congress; 6, 13 July Commonplace Book, 2, Murray Papers, Library of Congress.

30. Marshall Journal, 30 October 1797.

31. American Envoys to Timothy Pickering, 22 October and 8 November 1797, "Diplomatic Despatches, France," 6, Record Group 59; in the printed edition of the dispatches, all references to visits to the United States and landownership were omitted.

32. Van Staphorst and Hubbard was one of six houses that owned the Holland Land Company, in which Theophilus Cazenove was the head American agent. In the summer of 1797, James Marshall secured a loan from the firm to pay the interest on shares of the North American Land company. Statement of Bankruptcy Proceedings made by Robert Morris, 12 October 1801, Holland Land Company Papers, vol. 144, Gemeentearchief, Amsterdam.

33. John Marshall was also responsible for the loan. Holland Land Company Papers, vol. 144. Beveridge, *Marshall*, 2: 259, speculates that Hottinguer was connected with James Marshall. Winter, *Amsterdamsche Handel*, 2: 280, was the first to suggest the connection between the loan and the XYZ affair. For Pinckney's acquaintance with Hottinguer, see American Envoys to Timothy Pickering, 22 October 1797, "Diplomatic Despatches, France," 6, Record Group 59.

34. Joseph Pitcairn to Rufus King, 29 June 1798, King Papers, vol. 29, New-York Historical Society.

35. Szramkiewicz, *Les Régents*, pp. 168-76; it appears that Hottinguer returned to France after his marriage, however. Dossier on Hottinguer, 1793, F 7, 4744, Archives Nationales, Paris.

36. Winter, *Amsterdamsche Handel*, 2: 341, 344; Theophile Cazenove to Nicholas Hubbard, 12 February 1795, Holland Land Company Papers, vol. 300.

37. James Cazenove to Theophile Cazenove, 13 July 1796, Holland Land Company Papers, vol. 268.

38. A. de Cazenove, ed., *Journal de Madame de Cazenove d'Arlens* (Paris, 1903), pp. xxx-xxxi, 124-25.

39. Edwin R. Baldridge, "Talleyrand in the United States, 1794-1796," (Ph.D. dissertation, Lehigh University, 1963), pp. 100, 100-14. Baldridge argues that one land deal with Robert Morris fell through, which is confirmed by the Statement of Bankruptcy Proceedings by Robert Morris, 12 October 1801, Holland Land Company Papers, vol. 144. In a later article, "Talleyrand's Visit to Pennsylvania, 1794-1796," *Pennsyl-*

vania History 36 (1969): 159, Baldridge expands his argument: "Various authors have stated that Talleyrand participated in numerous land deals in America. Most of their remarks are nebulous, never citing exactly where the lands were situated, the size of the purchase, or the dates of the transactions. Furthermore, they never explain what he did with the lands he supposedly bought." For land around Cazenovia, New York, held in Cazenove's name from 1795-1830, see Cazenove, ed., *Journal de Cazenove d'Arlens*, pp. xxx-xxxi, 147n. Robert Morris wrote that Talleyrand did not want his American land purchases known in Europe, Morris to Theophile Cazenove, 23 October 1797, Robert Morris Papers, Library of Congress, Washington, D.C. For Talleyrand's land in Pennsylvania, see I. H. Le Combe tó Conderc, Brants, and Changuion, 28 April 1797, Brants Archive Gemeentearchief, Amsterdam, vol. 648; on the land held in Virginia with Charles de la Forest, see Geoffroy de Grandmaison, ed., *Correspondance du Comte de la Forest*, 8 vols. (Paris, 1905), 1: xii; for a loan to DuPont de Nemours on Kentucky lands, see Ambrose Saricks, *Pierre Samuel DuPont de Nemours* (Lawrence, Kansas, 1965), 305-6; for contemporary accounts that Talleyrand purchased American land, see Gerry to John Adams, 8 July 1779, Adams Papers; John Stone to Joseph Priestly, 12 February 1798, *Lettres au Docteur Priestly en Amerique* (London, 1798), p. 21.

40. Extract de la lettre de M. H. à notre maison, Hamburg, 20 March [1796], Brant Archives, vol. 648, Lüthy, *La Banque Protestante*, 2: 726n; Bellamy and Ricci to Campagnie de Ceres, 21 May, 16 August 1796; 6, 25 July, 26 September, 17 November 1797, Brant Archives, 648.

41. Szramkiewicz, *Les Régents*, p. 173.

42. Inventoire des Papiers, No. 25, Holland Land Company Papers, 108; Cazenove, ed., *Journal de Cazenove d'Arlens*, pp. xxx-xxxiii 147n; Peter J. Hugill, "A Small Town Landscape as a Sustained Gesture on the Part of a Dominant Social Group: Cazenovia, New York, 1794-1976," (Ph.D. diss., Syracuse University, 1977), pp. 513, 536-37.

43. LaCour-Gayet, *Talleyrand*, 1: 208, 229; the author identifies Ricci and Riccé as two different men, but see Fanny Burney Journal, 22 November 1798 in Joyce Hemlow, ed., *The Journals and Letters of Fanny Burney: Madame d'Arblay*, 6 vols. to date (Oxford, 1972-), 4: 172-73.

44. Theophile Cazenove to Nicholas Hubbard, 26 June 1796, Holland Land Company Papers, vol. 300.

45. LaCour-Gayet, *Talleyrand*, 1: 211; Szamkiewicz, *Les Régents*, 172; James Pitcairn to Rufus King, 28 September 1796, King Papers, vol. 25, New-York Historical Society. Pitcairn also stated that Talleyrand arrived in Paris on 20 September 1796.

46. Ibid.

47. Edouard L. Burnet, *Le Premier Tribunal Révolutionnaire Genvois* (Geneva, 1925), pp. 283, 305-7, 343, 356; John Q. Adams to Rufus King, 11 July 1798, Adams Papers.

48. Rufus Putnam to Twenty-Four Associates, 16 November 1790, Scioto Land Company Manuscripts, Historical Society of Pennsylvania, Philadelphia, Pennsylvania.

49. Beaumarchais to Samuel Sterett, 29 October 1796; Beaumarchais to Jean Chevallié, 29 October 1796; 26 June 1797, October 1797; Beaumarchais to Talleyrand, 17 October 1797; Hamilton to Beaumarchais, 13 February 1798, Private Archives, Paris.

50. Beaumarchais to Jean Chevallié, 9 October 1797; Cazenove to Beaumarchais, 26 October, 1798, Private Archives, Paris, Cazenove to Chevallié, 9 October 1797, Holland Land Company Papers, vol. 302.

51. [Boston] *Columbian Centinel*, 1 August 1798; according to the paper, Hauteval was involved in speculation in Europe with Boston partners, ibid., 5 September 1798.

52. John Marshall had the same situation on the American side with regard to his loans from Van Staphorst and Hubbard, arranged by Hottinguer, but Marshall held firm against giving in to France and felt willing to risk war, even though he needed capital to finance his land speculations. For material on the Marshall brothers' financial dealings in Europe in 1797, see Robert Morris to Henry Lee, 3 and 18 June, September 1797; Morris to Rawleigh Colston, 10 June and 14 October 1797; Morris to James Marshall, 29 May 1797, Morris Papers; Marshall to Mary Marshall, 3 July 1797, Marshall Papers, College of William and Mary, Williamsburg, Virginia.

53. William V. Murray reported that "Mr. Gerry's idea is to delay and gain time." Murray to John Q. Adams, 1 October 1797, Murray Papers, Pierpont Morgan Library; quote is from Gerry to Murray, 28 December 1797, Gratz Collection, Historical Society of Pennsylvania, Philadelphia, Pennsylvania. Gerry to John Adams, 3 July 1797, Adams Papers.

54. Charles Pinckney to Thomas Pinckney, 22 December 1797, Pickering Papers, vol. 8; Pinckney to Rufus King, 14 December 1797, King Papers, Library of Congress.

55. Alexandre Hauterive to Pierre Adet, 16 July 1797, Corr. Pol., Supplement, vol. 2.

56. Marshall to Charles Lee, 12-[27] October, "Diplomatic Despatches, France," 6, Record Group 59.

57. This woman has long been identified as Reine Philiberte de Varicourt, Marquisse de Villette, in whose apartments in Paris Marshall and Gerry lived. Theodore Lyman, *The Diplomacy of the United States*, 2 vols. (Boston, 1826), appears to be the first to make this claim, but James

Austin, *Life of Elbridge Gerry*, 2 vols. (Boston, 1828), 2: 202n, effectively rebuts Lyman's contention. Bowman, *Struggle for Neutrality*, p. 317, DeConde, *Quasi-War*, pp. 51-52, and Marvin Zahniser, *Charles Cotesworth Pinckney* (Chapel Hill, N.C., 1967), pp. 175-76, all identify the woman as Madame de Villette and describe her as an agent of Talleyrand. Zahniser and DeConde cite the letter of Mary Pinckney to Margaret Manigault, 9 March 1798, Manigault Family Papers, as their source. Mary Pinckney does discuss Madame de Villette in this letter, but with noteworthy errors concerning her children, marriage, age, and background. Later in the same letter Mary Pinckney also speaks of Madame de la Forest, whom both she and Margaret Manigault knew and who had approached Charles Pinckney at a party about three months before. Pinckney's account of the episode appears in American Envoys to Timothy Pickering, 24 December 1797, "Diplomatic Despatches, France," 6, Record Group 59.

58. King to Charles Pinckney, 24 December 1797; King to Elbridge Gerry, 24 December 1797, F 7, 4269, Archives Nationales, Paris; Pinckney to King, 27 December 1797, Pickering Papers, vol. 22.

59. American Envoys to Timothy Pickering, 24 December 1797, "Diplomatic Despatches, France," 6, Record Group 59; Beaumarchais to Pierre Bellamy, 21 December 1797; Bellamy to Beaumarchais, 26 December 1797, Private Archives, Paris.

60. Bellamy to Caron de Beaumarchais, 13 July 1798, Private Archives, Paris; Joseph Pitcairn to Rufus King, 6 July 1798, King Papers, vol. 29.

61. Winter, *Amsterdamsche Handel*, 2: 280.

62. Guyot, *Le Directoire*, p. 559n.

63. Jean Stern, *Belle et Bonne* (Paris, 1938), pp. 65-179; Gustave Desnoiresterres, *Voltaire et la Société au XVIIIe Siècle* 2d ed., 8 vols. (Paris, 1871-1876), 8: 92-102, 507-9.

64. Elbridge Gerry to Ann Gerry, 25 November 1797, Gerry Papers, Library of Congress, Washington, D.C.; for Marshall's more restrained description, see John Marshall to Mary Marshall, 27 November 1797, in *The Papers of John Marshall*, eds. William Stinchcombe and Charles Cullen, 3 vols. (Chapel Hill, N. C., 1979), 3: 299-301.

65. Marshall to Charles Pinckney [17 December 1797], Pinckney Papers, South Carolina Historical Society, Charleston, South Carolina; Mary Pinckney to Margaret Manigault, 9 March 1798, Manigault Family Papers.

66. DeConde, *Quasi-War*, pp. 51-52; Zahniser, *Pinckney*, p. 176.

67. See dossier 918 on "Marquisse de Villette, La Famille de Beaumarchais," F 7, 6152, Archives Nationales, Paris.

68. Gerry to John Adams, 8 July 1799, Adams Papers.

5

"A Member of the American Club"

As soon as the three envoys settled into their apartments, they visited and received calls from Americans who lived permanently in Paris. Members of the American community in Paris knew more about the French government's procedures and personnel than did the inexperienced envoys or their secretaries, and they freely offered their advice. In the controversy following the collapse of the negotiations, however, members of the American community found themselves accused of being more French than American in their loyalty. In 1797 the fear—and then the reality—of suspended payments from the French government, as well as threats of confiscation and explusion, motivated Americans in Paris to advocate a policy of restraint toward France, a position that put them at odds with many Federalists in the United States. A few ideologically inclined Americans found the prospect of war between two revolutionary republics unthinkable. Most Americans in Paris considered war both undesirable and unnecessary, at least until they had finished their business.

A week after the envoys officially presented themselves to Talleyrand in early October, Fulwar Skipwith predicted that it would be a while before the Americans would be received, because the Directory was very "busy." Joel Barlow explained that Talleyrand had hinted to the envoys to go slowly, but that advice was ignored. Nathaniel Cutting described the experience that he and many other Americans had at this point in the negotiations. "I have frequently had *unofficial* communications with some individuals connected in the French government; now and then I have had the honor to converse with the American Envoys."[1] Throughout the course of negotiations not only Barlow, Skipwith, and Cutting, but Richard Codman, Joseph Pitcairn, and Henry Middleton as well as other Americans presented themselves to offer their opinions to the envoys or, more often, to exert pressure on them.

Established in their lodgings, the envoys waited for Talleyrand to call them. First, they heard from Edward Church, a Bostonian and former American consul in Lisbon who had property and business interests in Paris. Church arranged a visit from the most acclaimed American in Paris, Thomas Paine, who presented the envoys with a sweeping neutrality plan which, if implemented, would have cur- tailed British domination of the seas. As Marshall suspected, Paine had consulted with Talleyrand before presenting his plan.[2] Another American, James Mountflorence, then approached Talleyrand's secretary, Baron d'Osmond, and the envoys in the role of inter- mediary. Mountflorence continued to act as a go-between for the French government and the envoys until Pinckney rebuked him. Realizing that he had used Mountflorence's services too often, in late November Talleyrand called upon Pitcairn to ascertain whether the envoys had changed their minds on advancing a loan to France.[3] Thus members of the American community figured in the early stage of the negotiations, no less than did Talleyrand's agents; when the negotiations failed, these Americans became objects of political controversy in the United States.

The reviving social life of Paris under the Directory offered Americans access to influential Frenchmen that the envoys and their secretaries lacked. While the envoys held no discussions with Talleyrand between October and March, other Americans saw him socially. In the last week of October, John Trumbull attended a dinner party at Madame de Staël's, where Talleyrand was also a guest. In his memoirs Trumbull recalled that Talleyrand instructed his hostess not to discuss politics, a prohibition that did not deter the foreign minister from insisting to Trumbull that the envoys must quickly grant a loan and forgo awaiting further instructions from Philadelphia. The very same evening that Talleyrand warned Trumbull, Pierre Bellamy called on Marshall to advise him of the consequences of delaying a settlement with France.[4] Talleyrand later gave a reception for Napoleon, including among the four hundred guests Gerry, Codman, Skipwith, and Middleton. But in

Mary Pinckney's opinion, Middleton's invitation to the affair could be attributed to the beauty of his twenty-one-year-old wife rather than any political considerations.[5]

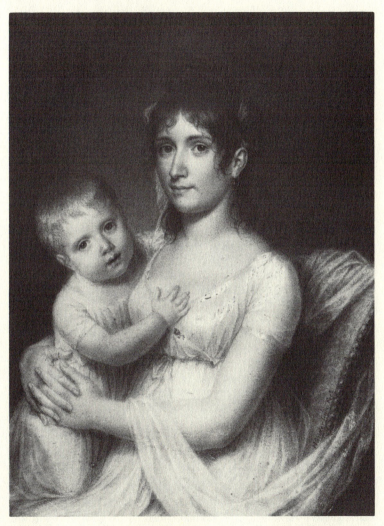

Figure 5. Mrs. Edward Church and Child by John Vanderlyn. *All rights reserved, The Metropolitan Museum of Art. Bequest of Ella Church Strobell, 1917.*

Because the envoys declined to call upon Talleyrand before they received official recognition, they particularly noted the opinions of Americans who had talked with the foreign minister informally. When Monroe was minister in 1795 and 1796, many Americans saw their compatriots in Paris as not only more French than American but as Jacobin as well. Charles Pinckney thought that the political character of the American community encouraged the growing division between Gerry and the other envoys. He complained that the "American Jacobins here pay him a great court," and that "every art is used by Talleyrand and French Americans here to detach Mr. Gerry from his colleagues."[6] Marshall shared Pinckney's assessment of many Americans in Paris, and stated after Church's visit that he was "An American I believe *by birth*," incorrectly adding in a display of pique, "who had been a consul of France."[7]

The prevailing characterization of Americans in Paris by those of Federalist sentiments was best stated by Mary Pinckney.

An american, a great friend of this government, told me yesterday that the french were determined to bring the english to their terms, and that to effect this they would take Hamburg if it were necessary, and continue to take our vessels, if by doing so they could humble England—friends or foes are alike to them—but I have not time to reason on these matters. They (such Americans) are amazingly fearful of hurting the feelings of this government, but are ready to find fault with their own—if an indecent paragraph against this government appears in our papers, where the press is free, they snort with anger and fear, but they can read violent tirades againt us in the french papers without any emotion—in short they would have their own government and its ministers to consider what may affect their fortunes in France and act accordingly.[8]

Marshall and Mary Pinckney both believed that financial self-interest inspired what they regarded as an overly zealous defense of French policy by Americans. The conventional wisdom of the eighteenth century held that financial interests served as the main-spring of political opinions, but in the case of Americans in Paris the nature and extent of these financial interests have gone unstudied. For instance, even a merchant trading heavily with France had many other commitments; neutrality meant trade with every nation, not just revolutionary ones. For a few Americans in Paris, ideology—revolutionary republicanism—had greater importance in shaping opinions than did economic interests. But in either event Americans in Paris played an important—and scarcely studied— role in the negotiations. An examination of the American community and how it affected the envoys' perception of France is fundamental to understanding the XYZ affair.

By 1796 the Directory had grown concerned about the number of British subjects traveling under American passports. The French government instructed James Monroe to report all Americans living in Paris and vouch for their citizenship. Monroe compiled periodic lists, now lost, which he submitted to the foreign office, which, in turn gave them to the police. In a covering letter Monroe reported between 100 and 150 American men of business who lived permanently in Paris.[9] By the end of 1797 the number had grown to more than 240 Americans in Paris. In addition, there were some twenty to forty American women who had married Frenchmen or moved with their husbands to France, including, as examples, Ruth Barlow, or Elizabeth Moore Barbé-Marbois, the American wife of the former chargé d'affaires in Philadelphia. Of the total number in 1797 there were about 150 merchants in Paris, which compares favorably with Monroe's lists for the year before.[10] A study for the 1814-1848 period estimates that about 300 Americans lived in or visited Paris each year during these three decades.[11] Apparently the American community in 1797-1798 was larger than at any time since the American Revolution.

The most conspicious occuption of these Americans (see Appendix) abroad was commerce. Excluded from trade with the British Empire after the American Revolution, these men compensated for the loss by expanding commerce with China, India, the French West Indies, and European ports. The opportunities presented by the disruptions of the French Revolution attracted these merchants, particularly the opportunity to carry supplies to the West Indies and export tropical foodstuffs and other goods from the French colonies there. A significant number of merchants, if not most, conducted a large part of their careers abroad. Given the special advantage of American neutrality, merchants found France a lucrative place of business. From Massachusetts came Nathaniel

Appleton, Walter Burling, Nathaniel Cutting, William Lee, and John and Richard Forbes. James Grubb and Jonathan Nesbitt, who were involved in the tobacco trade, had been in France before the French Revolution, as had John Gregorie of Petersburg. Merchants who held partnerships in larger houses included Richard Codman, associated with his brother John in Boston, George Murray of New York, and Henry Preble of Portland. Like many others, Daniel Ludlow of New York had lifelong international mercantile connections. Born in New York but related to prominent Amsterdam merchants, Ludlow went to the Netherlands for his apprenticeship before setting up business in New York. When he began trading extensively with the French West Indies in the early 1790s, he found it necessary to move to Paris to attempt to collect from the French government.[12]

The geographic area most strongly represented was New England. The Boston-Salem area alone accounted for more than sixty American merchants in Paris. Many reasons contributed to this region's preponderance, primarily its fishing and shipping interests and extensive trading connections with the West Indies. After the defeat of the French navy and the decimation of the French merchant marine in the early 1790s, many Boston merchants entered the carrying trade that centered in Bordeaux. Before the French Revolution Bordeaux had handled close to half the French foreign trade, largely from Haiti. At the time of the American Revolution only a few Americans had entered this commerce, but by 1793 there were well over sixty merchants and sea captains at Bordeaux, and in the period from 1795 to 1812 the number of American merchants there rarely dropped below thirty.[13] Having been a merchant in Marblehead, Elbridge Gerry had a greater circle of acquaintances in the American community than did either of his colleagues. He had previously known at least fifteen Boston merchants now living in Paris.

Merchants found American citizenship such a valued commodity that the French government rightly suspected many Scotsmen of posing as Americans. Neutrality was prized for its protection against Great Britain and for the access to the British market denied other Europeans. Dutch merchants, moreover, had been stifled by the French occupation, while the Americans could still use French ports as well as import scarce goods through the Dutch ports of Amsterdam and Rotterdam. Hamburg's neutral status also made it an attractive port for Americans. Barlow's wealth, for example, derived from importing foodstuffs through Hamburg into France. [14] Rumor held that Benjamin Hichborn of Boston—others attributed that task to his partner James Swan—was asked by the Committee of Public Safety to export the crown jewels and sell them on the European market. [15] For American merchants, neutrality enhanced their financial interests, provided they could impel the French goverment to pay for goods delivered, whereas war with France would destroy a temporarily advantageous situation.

The size of the American community had grown rapidly after the outbreak of war between France and Great Britain in 1793. In 1791 William Short found fewer than 20 Americans to celebrate 4 July. [16] Five years later, close to 100 Americans attended Monroe's controversial celebration, at which the host was said to have allowed criticism of President Washington's policies. [17] By 1797 the number of Americans had continued to increase. From the compiled list we can identify 147 merchants, 22 ship captains, and 22 land agents. Of the merchants 15 had contracts with the French government for supplies.

The immediate reason for the increase in the number of merchants was the food shortages in France in 1793-1794 and in Haiti from 1791 on. When the shortages in France became obvious, the Committee of Public Safety contracted with James Swan to send American foodstuffs to France as a form of payment for what the United States owed France from the American Revolution. Swan returned to the United States and efficiently arranged for the dispatch of 113 ships to France within a seven-month period. [18] Forty ships left from Boston, New York, and Philadelphia, and the remainder embarked from southern ports. The leading merchants contracted by Swan included Samuel Higginson, Samuel and Thomas Perkins of Boston, James Murray of New York, Donald Steward and Sons of Baltimore, and Mason and Fenwick of Georgetown. The major firm commissioned for food shipments to the French West Indies was Z. Coopman and Sons of Baltimore. [19]

Swan promised a quick profit to all merchants, and in a period of rapidly rising food prices in the United States—caused partly by his contracts—he argued that a 25 percent profit per ship was not unreasonable. When French officials complained that Swan had hired pro-English merchants, meaning that they had supported the Jay Treaty, to ship goods to France, he replied, "The Secrets of business is Sacred in a merchants hands, let his politics be English or French." He added, "They are like a band of Thieves: merchants are always faithful to one another."[20]

Complications arose, however, in collecting from the French government after the ships arrived in France. Other American ships were confiscated by municipal embargoes or detained so long that the captains could legitimately claim damages. Not surprisingly, the American community in 1797-1798 included a number of merchants seeking payment from Swan's contracts. Two of Higginson's sons, two Murray brothers, Walter Burling and William Lee for Thomas and Samuel Perkins, and Coopman all sought to arrange for payment on goods shipped two or three years before.

Another notable group of claimants in Paris included merchants who had had ships confiscated in the embargo at Bordeaux or in French privateering raids in the West Indies. At least forty ships were impounded at Bordeaux in 1793, and four years later at least a dozen merchants remained in Paris still trying to collect. According to an admittedly incomplete source, at least 220 American ships had been captured in the West Indies by the end of 1797.[21] A few in the American community, notably Skipwith and Mountflorence, served as agents for their compatriots, pressing dozens of American claims. Both these men purchased American claims for nominal amounts and then sought redress, as well as quick profit, in France's unpredictable legal system.[22]

Following the creditors, the next identifiable group consisted of the agents of American land companies. Distinctions between merchants, suppliers to the French armies, and agents for land companies are difficult, however, because some residents, such as Barlow and Mountflorence, combined all activities. Gerry's first secretary, Bossenger Foster, Jr., of Boston, accepted the position because it offered him a passport to Paris, where he planned to sell some New York lands of his uncle Andrew Craigie.[23] If a Frenchman wished to secure his funds against the revolution's vicissitudes, he had ample opportunities to purchase land almost anywhere in the United States. Perhaps appropriately, visitors to Barlow's second-story apartment during his first years in Paris had to pass through a gambling parlor on the first floor. The odds there might have been better than those in investing in American real estate.

Barlow, moreover, was just one of many selling American land in Paris at this time. For upstate New York purchases in what was labeled the rich Genesee lands, a Frenchman could see Oliver Phelps, Jr., James Wadsworth, or James Marshall, the envoy's brother. For Virginia and Kentucky lands, Louis Marshall, another of John's brothers, John Brockenbourgh, Samuel Blackden, and Samuel Hopkins offered the choicest parcels on the American frontier. Mountflorence acted as the Blount brothers' representative for lands all over the American Southwest. For Maine lands at a pittance, a desperate Frenchman needed only to call upon Joseph Waldo, Benjamin Hichborn, or Hichborn's stepson, Samuel Andrews. Mark Leavenworth, Jr., of Hartford, James LeRay, a naturalized American, and Louis d'Autremont, Talleyrand's secretary, posing as a Canadian who had been naturalized in the United States, offered vast lands in central and northern New York. By only slight exaggeration we can say that an American in Paris in these years stood ready and willing to offer the French a unique opportunity to invest in unsettled and frequently worthless American lands.[24]

Residents of Paris provided leadership in protecting American interests in France. When Hezekiah Pierpont wanted to protest the confiscation of his ship and cargo at Nantes in 1797, he sent a copy of the judgment against him to the American envoys. But he also sent copies to a number of other Americans in Paris, and their names suggest a ranking within the American community, a community led by merchants. Pierpont dispatched his plea to Skipwith, John Mitchell of New York, Joseph Pitcairn, Joseph Sands, Daniel Parker, Richard Codman, Mark Leavenworth, Joel Barlow, and John Dabney.[25]

The activities of some of these merchants deserve further scrutiny. A leader less prominent than Paine and Barlow but nevertheless important was Richard Codman. Codman sold furniture as a lucrative sideline in the midst of revolution, while conducting an importing business, as a good neutral, in French and Dutch ports as well as Hamburg.[26] His parties, described by Mary Pinckney as the most lavish of the time, were well attended by Frenchmen and Americans. These affairs offered a combination of dining, concerts, and dancing. Codman had purchased a townhouse elegantly "finished and furnished," which he sold to Talleyrand in 1799.[27] On the outskirts of Paris he also bought a chateau, which he rebuilt at a cost of 4,360,000, some odd francs, an extraordinary sum, even in depreciated currency, for investment in a second house.

Codman's leadership in the American community did not long endure, however. Hearing of Codman's activities in Paris, Alexander Baring, whose London banking house was connected with Codman's in Boston, noted that his financial condition would remain secure, for brother John kept Richard on a tight rein and would not allow him to go deeply in debt or become affected by the French government.[29] On both counts, Baring was mistaken. Codman was closely associated with the French government and intervened constantly in French-American dealings, being the American most trusted by both Talleyrand and Gerry near the end of the negotiations in the spring of 1798. Not surprisingly, within three years John Codman had to travel to Paris to deal with Richard's bankruptcy. Around 1802 Richard Codman departed Paris after more than a decade of business, social, and political life, leaving behind his much-mentioned mistress, his chateau, and his elegant parties, to die a respectable bachelor in Boston a few years later.

After Codman's fortunes fell, Daniel Parker emerged as a leader of the American community. Parker, who had had extensive business with the French government, particularly Rochambeau's army, during the American Revolution, moved to Paris in the 1780s to conduct his own business interests and handle Baring's banking affairs there. Constantly overspending his income, Parker became involved in shadowy schemes to wrest Louisiana from Spain in 1792 and West Florida from Spain in 1810. Parker, Barlow, Leavenworth, and Skipwith were the Americans most active in these dubious ventures to encourage France to dismantle the Spanish empire for their own enrichment.[30]

Like Codman, Parker lived on a lavish scale—successfully, since he remained in Paris until the 1830s. Parker speculated in confiscated lands of émigrés, at one time owning three different chateaux close to Paris, including one once belonging to Madame de Pompadour.[31] Again like Codman, Parker showed an inclination for morals not favored in Boston. He lived openly with the wife of his fellow American, Henry Preble, an arrangement much remarked upon by New Englanders but rarely by Southerners. He dispatched Preble for long periods in which to transact important business.[32]

Americans speculated widely in French and Dutch funds, a practice in which a misjudgment sent Jesse Putnam of Boston to jail. More fortunate was John Trumbull, for he achieved financial security through speculation. Yet the more persistent interest lay in the purchase of confiscated estates, as we have seen in Codman's and Parker's acquisitions.[33] Jonathan Russell, a Bostonian and longtime resident in Paris, purchased a chateau seven or eight miles from Paris. For the building and eighteen acres of land, Russell paid 200,000 francs in specie or hard currency, and 132,500 in greatly depreciated assignats, the currency of the government. An envious Thomas Perkins called Russell's acquisition "A great spec[ulation]." Three days later Perkins joined Russell and John Higginson on an expedition to consider the purchase of another chateau, one formerly owned by a member of the royal family.[34]

Other Americans purchased houses in Paris. Following the practice of Monroe, Skipwith, Mountflorence, and Barlow, Mark Leavenworth acquired an expensive townhouse on the Champs Élysées, while Joseph Sands and Henry Sadler of New York bought the Hotel Bourbon-Conde. At one time Skipwith owned five town houses on the Left Bank. On the Right Bank, William Temple Franklin purchased seventy building lots, the proceeds of which allowed him to continue his dissipated life in Paris. The secular American creed notwithstanding, Franklin owned an abby in Paris, while Skipwith invested in a large one near Caens, for which he paid a half million francs. Edward Church and William Rogers won several houses in the national lottery, as did other Americans—perhaps an indication that Frenchmen wanted Americans to assume official titles to safeguard these properties. William Short, for example, did this for property of Madame de la Rochefoucauld.[35]

In addition to merchants, the American community included an identifiable group of students, intellectuals, and artists. We can identify five students and at least five more who spent time in Paris during their travels in Europe, including Thomas B. Adams, the president's son. These few students offer little pattern, except perhaps for a lingering connection between the Huguenots of South Carolina and French schooling. Mary Pinckney had attended a school in Paris during the American Revolution, as had Margaret Manigault, daughter of the American diplomat Ralph Izard. Two of Izard's sons, Ralph and George, attended French schools in the Paris area during the years 1797-1798, as did John Higginson of Boston. Also from Charleston, under Charles Pinckney's none-too-watchful eye, were States Rutledge and Henry Middleton.

Another American student was John Vanderlyn of Kingston, New York. Acting on the advice of Gilbert Stuart and under the patronage of Aaron Burr, Vanderlyn arrived in Paris in 1795. The first American admitted to the École des Beaux Arts, he studied under André Vincent and also developed a friendship with another instructor, the artist Jacques Louis David. After first rooming with a Belgian art student, in 1797 Vanderlyn moved into Fulwar Skipwith's hotel and lived with the American consul. There he became acquainted with Barlow, Robert Fulton, Codman, and Madame de Villette. He began to make himself " a good deal known among the Americans by making a few little portraits" of the envoys' social circle. Among the Americans whom Vanderlyn painted were members of the Church family, Fulton, Skipwith, George Gibbs, Jr., Parker, Gerry, and probably John Marshall and Madame de Villette.[36]

Yet another intimate member of the American community was Robert Fulton, who arrived in Paris after studying under the artist Benjamin West in London. By then describing himself as an engineer, Fulton divided his time between portraiture, including as his subjects several Americans and Madame de Villette's daughter, and devising mechanical inventions. Just as the negotiations were collapsing, the Directory awarded Fulton a patent on canal equipment. Aided by Barlow, with whom he lived, Fulton began experiments to develop a self-propelled torpedo, a venture that ultimately proved unsuccessful.[37]

A few Americans in Paris simply preferred life there to that in the United States. Generally they also expressed a strong distaste for

Figure 6. John Vanderlyn, a self-portrait, circa 1815. *All rights reserved, The Metropolitan Museum of Art. Bequest of Ann S. Stephens in the name of her mother Mrs. Ann S. Stephens, 1918.*

Great Britain. Mary Pinckney argued that her fellow Charlestonian Henry Middleton did not live a dissipated life "in a philosophical sense."

Mr. Middleton hates London, & England, & loves Paris. He says it is the most agreeable place in the world. Every odd day he attends Charles lectures from ten till near two, & immediately after Fourcroys lectures on chemistry from 2 till four. He makes notes—he corrects them—he learns french & italian—he finds out pictures—he buys a few—he sometimes goes to a subscription ball, & often to plays—he amuses himself, not in a disscipated, but in a philosophical manner.[38]

At another time she spoke of Middleton's purchasing thirty engravings by Raphael for a pittance.[39] Not surprisingly, Middleton remained in Paris for a number of years, as did another of Mary Pinckney's kinsmen, Charles Pinckney Horry.[40]

   William Vernon, Jr., was the son of a well-known Newport merchant who had extensive supply contracts with the French. Arriving in Paris in the 1790s, the younger Vernon could not resist the attractions of Paris. Travelers to France carried his father's repeated appeals that he return home. But instead of going home, he stayed in Paris, investing in shipping, buying American shipping claims, and acquiring French property. Not for almost three decades did William Vernon, Jr., report home to Newport, carrying with him a huge art collection acquired during the revolutionary and Napoleonic years in Paris.[41]

   Middleton, Vernon, and other Americans in Paris exploited the vast art collections brought to Paris, both legally and illegally, to make extensive acquisitions. The confiscations of nobles' estates had provided a glut on the art market that allowed Americans to build collections at exceptionally low prices. Joseph Smith, brother of South Carolina Federalist William Loughton Smith, collected "73 cases of valuable paintings—near 3,000 gems—some valuable statues, real antiques—some copies, which he himself superintended, of the most renowned statues of Rome, Florence, and Naples of colossal size." According to Mary Pinckney, Smith saw his art collection as something with which "to gratify his countrymen."[42] George Gibbs, Jr., whose son was to write histories of the

Washington and Adams administrations, purchased a mineral collection containing over 12,000 samples. Gibbs bought a large part of the collection from the family of Gigot d'Orcy, a member of the Farmers General, who had been guillotined.[43] Returning to the United States, Gibbs lent, and later sold, his collection to Yale, thus forming the basis of the university's mineral collection.

The best-known example of an American delving into the revolution's art treasures is John Trumbull. At the suggestion of his compatriot in London, Benjamin West, Trumbull decided to exploit the great quantities of confiscated and purloined art available in Paris. Financially supported by the ubiquitous Daniel Parker, Trumbull commissioned the Paris art dealer LeBrun to provide advice on which works of art to buy.[44] LeBrun had the knowledge and experience from which to recommend choices, since he had also been commissioned by the French government to produce an inventory of the art that it had acquired in these years.[45] Trumbull purchased seven paintings from Peter Constantin, an American merchant at Bordeaux, and in later exchanges in London sold more than a hundred paintings. In addition, Trumbull kept fifteen paintings for himself, which he gave to Yale, and acquired fifty more for Parker's private collection. Trumbull concentrated on Italian and Flemish works, because neither the British nor the Americans preferred eighteenth-century French art. Among the works Trumbull acquired in Paris were paintings by Rembrandt, Van Dyck, Poussin, Reubens, and Titian.

Americans speculating in art in Paris at this time introduced many valued European works of art to the United States. In 1804 Trumbull advertised an exhibition of his collection in New York, "which consists principally of Original Paintings of eminent ancient masters." At the opening exhibit of the Pennsylvania Academy of Fine Arts in 1806, Joseph Smith donated and loaned a number of his works. Robert Fulton also presented the Philadelphia exhibit with some of his own creations as well as a few that he had purchased in Paris.[46] The Boston Athenaeum asked William Vernon to allow some of his collections to form an entire exhibition in 1830, just after Vernon's return from Paris. From his vast collection, he sent dozens of works, representing more than two dozen European artists of the fifteenth through the eighteenth centuries.[47] Few

Figure 7. John Trumbull, a self-portrait, 1801. *Courtesy of Wadsworth Atheneum, Hartford, Connecticut.*

Americans visiting the art exhibitions of the time realized that these newly acquired cultural trappings could be attributed to the armies and guillotines of the hated Jacobins.

In addition to art acquisitions, Americans frequently speculated in the furniture market. Gouverneur Morris and James Swan led in buying confiscated furniture at public auctions and sending it back to the United States. Like many Americans in Paris, Mary Pinckney constantly searched for bargains to be shipped to Charleston for herself and her friends. The most spectacular enterprise was Swan's. In his contract with the Committee of Public Safety to import foodstuffs to France, he was allowed to select pieces of confiscated furniture for shipment back to the United States. Swan received priority to select the furniture before it was displayed at public auctions. Acting with him were Captains Stephen Clough and Joseph Rogers, who supervised the transportation of two shiploads of the finest French furniture back to Massachusetts.[48] As in the art market, Americans greatly increased their holdings of European luxuries, as the revolution and plundering armies wreaked havoc on the French nobility.

Another American. Thomas Melville, Jr., moved between the worlds of art, banking, and diplomacy. Born in Boston, the son of the federal excise collector there, Melville went to France at the age of seventeen in 1794. He opened a banking business in Paris, speculating for James Tisdale, a Boston merchant; he remained in Paris until 1811.[49] Melville established connections with prominent French bankers, and not only neutrality but banking seemed to afford more than the usual degree of protection against the shifting governments of the revolution.

Melville's first mission in the service of French imperialism involved helping to pack and ship more than four hundred paintings and works of art as spoils of victory from Napoleon's triumph in Italy. He then entered the negotiations between the French and the British at Lille at the behest of Barras in the late summer of 1797.[50] Melville's mission at Lille was to persuade Lord Malmesbury of Great Britain that a bribe would make Talleyrand and members of the Directory amenable to breaking the deadlocked negotiations. He asked for the same sum that Jean Conrad Hottinguer requested from the Americans when he told them that £50,000 was the standard amount for such transactions. The explanation for the use of the bribe was also similar: Talleyrand would distribute it carefully among the Directory to win a majority for a peaceful policy toward Great Britain. Melville's growing notoriety in these dealings led to his being one of the two Americans—Joesph Pitcairn was the other—whose arrest was ordered in the summer of 1797.[51]

When the negotiations at Lille collapsed, two days before Hot-tinguer and Bellamy first approached the American envoys, Melville left for London, where he presented his case to William Pitt and members of the cabinet. Unsuccessful, Melville then departed for Amsterdam for business unknown. It may be surmised, how-ever, that his business there had to do with Dutch loans, since French bribery offers made to Hamburg, Great Britain, and the United States were linked with purchasing Dutch loans at more than double the market rate. Not by mere coincidence did Hub-bard, Hottinguer, and Bellamy have banking interests in Amster-dam. Melville returned from Amsterdam to Paris in late 1797, and apparently his friends were powerful enough to prevent his arrest. Later his nephew, Herman Melville, wrote that his uncle was "of an enterprising and sanguine temperament," and while in Europe "he engaged in various tempting ventures, for which the wars then convulsing the continent gave frequent opportunity."[52] The same could be applied to a good many members of the American com-munity in Paris.

An American newly arrived in Paris in 1797 could rely on a network of informal associations to put him in touch with his compatriots. He would most likely put up at the Hotel États-Unis, the most popular hotel for Americans in the years after the Ameri-can Revolution. Americans had also established an informal club in Paris, the Decadi Club, which met in one of the better restaurants in Paris in the Palais Royal. Thomas Perkins spoke of twenty people attending a long luncheon there in 1795.[53] Victor DuPont described his experience in Paris in 1801:

I was received [as] a member of the American Club. About 30 of the Americans now in Paris dine together 3 times a month at one of the Restauranteurs of the Palais Royal. The diner is dressed quite in the American style; and there are rules observed, as in these societies in America, where we fancy ourselves transported for a few hours and to our great satisfaction.[54]

Joshua Gilpin of Philadelphia offers a good picture of a new arrival's introduction to the American community in Paris. He reached Paris in November 1797 to protest the seizure of cargo by

a French privateer in the West Indies. On his first day he visited the
Pinckneys and Gerry, and on his second determined details about
his passport, later spending the evening with the Barlows, Robert
Fulton, and Samuel Hopkins, at the Barlow's apartment. Two days
later he went to the theater with Gerry, Barlow, and Codman. A
week after arriving in Paris, he dined with the Pinckneys for the
second time, joined by Codman and the Henry Middletons. Within
a ten-day period he also called upon the Church family, Nathaniel
Cutting, and Joseph Waldo. Despite his efforts, Gilpin was not
successful in pressing the claim made on behalf of himself and his
brother against the French government. In 1803, however, he was
to receive an award from a commission that distributed compensa-
tion from money set aside from the Louisiana Purchase. But in the
meantime he continued his trip, going on to Bordeaux to arrange
mercantile details with American houses there. As did many other
Americans in Europe, he visited Voltaire's house outside Geneva,
having first talked with Madame de Villette, whose husband had
purchased the house after Voltaire's death.[55]

Gilpin could readily locate many Americans because they con-
gregated in one area, in a pattern of residence comparable to that of
American loyalists in London during the American Revolution.[56]
On Rue de Bac, Madame de Saint-Hilaire, probably the wife of a
royalist army officer in exile in the United States, ran a boarding
house where Barlow and Robert Fulton lived for two years. The
year before, William Lee and seven other Americans had had
rooms there.[57] The American envoys had lodgings within a few
blocks, and other Americans living close by included Skipwith, the
Churches, and James Thayer of Charleston. This concentration of
Americans on the Left Bank was possible because an estimated
one-third to one-half of the buildings in this section of Paris
changed owners in the early years of the revolution. Barlow,
Skipwith, Church, Thayer, and Griffith were among the Americans
purchasing houses on the Left Bank for speculative purposes.[58]

The political opinions of Americans in Paris, although controversial, followed the same pattern as those of Federalists and
Republicans in the United States. The best approach in understanding these political beliefs is to divide the American community
between those who voted for Adams and those who voted for

Jefferson in the 1796 election. The Jeffersonians were probably a majority, a majority that became larger after 1800. Party alignment has greater value in understanding the American community than other attributes such as distinctions between governmental contractors and creditors, which cannot be solidly linked with political outlook.

Among the Federalists who can be identified are Francis Childs, William Constable, Theodore Lyman, Jr., George Gibbs, Jr., Joshua Gilpin, Thomas W. Griffith, and James Wadsworth. Richard Codman, who had Federalist leanings, worked consistently to keep negotiations open and to demonstrate to his countrymen that the French truly desired peace. Another Federalist who had a prominent role as go-between was James Mountflorence, as we have discussed.

The Republicans in Paris included Thomas Paine, Joel Barlow, Nathaniel Cutting, William Short, Fulwar Skipwith, and Robert Fulton. A number of characteristics distinguish these men from their Federalist counterparts in Paris. Many had lived in Paris longer, most were friends or correspondents of Thomas Jefferson, more lived or moved on the fringes of the intellectual and artistic world, and most had signed the petition supporting James Monroe at the time of his recall in 1796. Some Federalists, to be sure, had also signed the petition for Monroe. Among Republicans, Skipwith in particular had worked to prevent the election of Adams and submitted his resignation when he learned the election results.[59] He had encouraged Monroe to remain in Paris even after the arrival of his successor, Charles C. Pinckney, in hopes that Jefferson would win and reappoint Monroe. Skipwith and other Republicans in Paris assumed, to a much greater degree than did their leader in Philadelphia, that only Jeffersonians would be able to establish peace between the two nations.

At its heart the Jeffersonian group did have a strain of radical republicanism. Barlow and Paine are the most obvious examples. Both were dedicated, as was Monroe, to a European-wide revolution. They particularly wished to see Great Britain humbled, reshaped by revolution. The republics of France and the United States held mystical meaning for these men despite instances of oppression and national aggrandizement by these nations. Though constantly disappointed, they rarely lost faith; they readily declared

Figure 8. Robert Fulton, a self-portrait, 1807. *Courtesy of Nelson Gallery-Atkins Museum, Kansas City, Missouri. (Nelson Fund).*

Robespierre a blood-thirsty tyrant and later, Napoleon a military despot, but their disenchantment was with the damage these men did to revolutionary republicanism, not with the ideal itself.

The radical Jeffersonians in Paris took alarm at the supposed monarchical tendencies of Washington and the Federalists. In 1796 Paine had published his latest appraisal of Washington: a coward, a liar, a betrayer of friends;[60] John Adams, whom John

Eustace called an "apostate pedant," came to personify the enemy at home because of his refusal to condemn aristocrats categorically, his lack of faith in the French Revolution, and his victory over Thomas Jefferson.[61] Americans of this persuasion could not believe that France itself, more than the Federalists, had endangered republicanism. That France had overthrown the oligarchic republics of Venice, Switzerland, and the Netherlands was not conceded. The vision of republicanism above nationalism was not easily cast aside.

A Boston Federalist editor understood the chasm between the Jeffersonians in Paris and the Federalists in the United States. He printed one of Timothy Pickering's slashing attacks on supposed French treachery under a headline of his own making: "Frenchmen! COSMOPOLITANS—Read with Care the Following."[62] It was the cosmopolitan conception held by Jefferson and a number of his followers that most disturbed the Federalists. Americans in Paris, whether the Federalist Codman or the Jeffersonian Barlow, displayed a cosmopolitanism increasingly unpopular at home.

The moral views of Americans in Paris seemed in conflict with traditions in the United States. An obvious example is the frequent mention of mistresses in diaries and letters written in Paris. Such conduct was not only practiced but was seen and acknowledged. The role of art offers another example. When the American Academy of Arts in New York sent John Vanderlyn to Paris to obtain copies of outstanding statues, it then voted to hire someone to produce fig leaves for the works of art. In her teens Harriet Manigault wrote that her relatives, particularly her uncle, Joseph A. Smith, placed sheets in front of European paintings before she and her two sisters visited his house.[63] Americans' constant attendance at the theater and opera in Paris showed that they, too, enjoyed frivolity, given the opportunity. Imports from Europe, greatly increased by the gains that Americans reaped from the French Revolution, introduced in the United States the art, furniture, and clothes of an upper-class culture; they also raised the specter of luxury. To many, luxury marked the first sign of a nation's decay and corruption, as both political leaders and the clergy had so often reminded Americans since the start of their own revolution. Stern, austere republicanism could not blend with cosmopolitanism. In the United States Americans were growing disdainful of any but their own standards in politics, art, or morals—of any ideal other than the American version of revolution and government. This judgment entered the complex reaction to the American community in Paris, which bore the stigma of Jacobinism and cosmopolitanism with little regard for the meaning of those two words. But in the context of 1798 both terms had deep political connotations.

Figure 9. Sarah Russell Church by John Vanderlyn. *All rights reserved, The Metropolitan Museum of Art. Bequest of Ella Church Strobell, 1917.*

Marshall and Pinckney, who openly sought and admired the worldly delights of Paris while deploring them, correctly perceived what so many of their countrymen did not—that Americans in Paris often failed to acknowledge the naked power politics underlying French actions. Because Americans in Paris sought reconciliation between the two nations, they seemed not to acknowledge the obstacles facing the envoys. The hostility with which Marshall and Pinckney responded to Americans' suggestions of a milder policy toward France indicated their own growing frustration over the deadlocked negotiations and the apparent impossibility of reaching their goal. Rather than closing all avenues of informal negotiations, however—as they had vowed they would do—Marshall and Pinckney rebuffed overtures made by Americans but continued to deal with Talleyrand's agents, Caron de Beaumarchais and Pierre S. DuPont, during their last four months in Paris. By their own choice these two envoys, unlike Gerry, chose to judge any changes in the French position only through Talleyrand's chosen intermediaries.

Notes

1. Quote is from Nathaniel Cutting to Pierce Butler, 13 March 1798, Letterbook, 1793-1798, Nathaniel Cutting Papers, Massachusetts Historical Society, Boston, Massachusetts, italics in original; Fulwar Skipwith to James Monroe, 20 October 1797, James Monroe Papers, Library of Congress, Washington, D.C.; Joel Barlow to James Cathalan, 29 October 1797, Barlow Papers, Harvard University, Cambridge, Massachusetts.

2. John Marshall Journal, 11 October 1797, Pickering Papers, Massachusetts Historical Society, Boston, Massachusetts; Thomas Paine to Talleyrand, 28, 30 September 1797, Correspondance Politique, États-Unis, vol. 48, Archives du Ministère des Affairs Étrangéres, Paris (hereafter, Corr. Pol.).

3. Marshall Journal, 14 October, 6, 7, 22-28 November 1797.

4. Ibid.,, 26 October 1797; Notebook, November 1797, Rufus King Papers, vol. 73 New-York Historical Society, New York, New York. For Trumbull's confusion of the two interviews with Talleyrand, see Theodore Sizer, ed., *The Autobiograpy of John Trumbull* (New Haven, Conn., 1953), pp. 221, 222.

5. *Salem Gazette*, 27 March 1798; Mary Pinckney to Margaret Manigault, 23 January 1798, Manigault Family Papers, University of South Carolina, Columbia, South Carolina.

6. Charles C. Pinckney to Rufus King, 14 December 1797, Rufus King Papers, Library of Congress, Washington, D.C.; Pinckney to Thomas Pinckney, 22 February 1798, Pickering Papers, vol. 22.

7. Marshall Journal, 11 October 1797, italics in original.

8. Mary Pinckney to Margaret Manigault, 6 December 1797, Manigault Family Papers.

9. James Monroe to Minister of Foreign Affairs, 12 May 1795, 4 April, 14 May 1796, Monroe Papers; Comité de Sûreté général to Monroe, 26 August 1795, F 7, 2205, Archives Nationales, Paris; Commissioner of Police to the Directory, 29 July, 2, 23, August 1795, F⁷ Register, 80, ibid.

10. More than one hundred names of Americans are included in passport issues in 1797-1798 in F 7, 642, Archives Nationales; a petition of support for Monroe was signed by sixty-nine Americans and is printed in James Monroe, *A View of the Conduct of the Executive* (Philadelphia, 1797), pp. 400-01; a list of Americans in Paris giving money for imprisoned seamen is in [Philadelphia] *Gazette and Universal Daily Advertiser*, 22 December 1798; also "United States Consuls in Paris," 1, Record Group 59, National Archives, Washington, D.C.

Diaries by Americans in Paris include Thomas Perkins, Journal, Thomas H. Perkins Papers, Massachusetts Historical Society, Boston, Massachusetts; Diary Book, William Lee, Lee-Palfrey Papers, Library of Congress, Washington, D.C.; Joshua Gilpin Journal, vol. 36, Joshua and Thomas Gilpin Papers, Pennsylvania Historical and Museum Commission, Harrisburg, Pennsylvania; for Thomas Griffith, see Elizabeth Latimer, *My Scrap-Book of the French Revolution* (Chicago, 1898); Letitia A. Humphreys, ed., "Diary of Clement Humphries," *Pennsylvania Magazine of History and Biography* 32 (1908): 34-53; Beatrix Davenport, ed., *A Diary of the French Revolution*, 2 vols. (Boston, 1939); for other diaries that mention Americans, see Victor DuPont, *Journey to France and Spain*, ed. Charles W. David (Ithaca, N.Y., 1961); J. B. T. Bury and J. C. Barry, eds., *An Englishman in Paris; The Journal of Bertie Greatheed* (London, 1953).

For spoliation claims, see "Debts Due by France to Americans," 23 September 1800, William Davie Papers, North Carolina State Archives, Raleigh, N.C.; "American Commission, Paris, 1803," Record Group 76, National Archives; *French Spoliations Prior to the Year 1800*, HR Doc. 182, 24th Cong., 1838; *French Spoliations to 1800*, HR Report 116, 27th Cong., 1841.

The best secondary works include Yvon Bizardel, *Les Américains à Paris pendant la Révolution* (Paris, 1972); Yvon Bizardel, "French Estates, American Landlords," trans. Florence Yorke, *Apollo* 101 (1975): 108-15; John Alger, *Englishmen in the French Revolution* (London, 1889); John

Alger, *Paris, 1789-1794* (London, 1902); Clifford Shipton, ed., *Biographical Sketches of Those Who Attended Harvard*, 17 vols. (Boston, 1873-1975), vols. 15, 16, and 17; Franklin B. Dexter, ed., *Biographical Sketches of Graduates of Yale, 1778-1792* (New York, 1907).

11. Guillaume de Berteir de Sauvigny, "American Travelers in France, 1814-1848," in *Diplomacy in an Age of Nationalism*, eds. Nancy Barker and Marvin Brown, Jr. (The Hague, 1971), p. 11.

12. For Ludlow, see Allen Johnson and Dumas Malone, eds., *Dictionary of American Biography*, 31 vols. (New York, 1931), 11: 490-91.

13. Protest of Embargo and Names of Ships and Captains, 12 October 1793, Petition of American Merchants at Bordeaux in favor of Isaac C. Barnet, 20 July 1801, "Despatches of United States Consuls in Bordeaux," 1, Record Group 59, National Archives; DuPont, *Journey to France and Spain, 1801*, pp. 92-93n, 96-97n; Paul Butel, *Les négociations bordelais, L'Europe et les Iles au XVIIIᵉ Siècle* (Paris, 1974), p. 333.

14. Robert Durden, "Joel Barlow in the French Revolution," *William and Mary Quarterly* 8 (1951): 348-49; James Woodress, *A Yankee's Odyssey: The Life of Joel Barlow* (Philadelphia, 1958), p. 149.

15. Bizardel, *Américains à Paris*, pp. 150, 247: Julian V. Niemcewicz, *Under Their Vine and Fig Tree*, ed. and trans. Metchie J. C. Budka (Elizabeth, N.J., 1965), p. 171.

16. William Short to John B. Cutting, 28 June 1791, William Short Papers, Library of Congress, Washington, D.C.

17. Perkins Journal, 14 June 1795.

18. Howard Rice, Jr., "James Swan: Agent of the French Republic," *New England Quarterly* 10(1937): 484-86.

19. Shipping records are in Corr. Pol. États-Unis, Supplement, vol. 21, Archives du Ministère des Affaires Étrangéres.

20. James Swan to Pierre Adet, 12 August 1796, ibid., vol. 22.

21. Protest of Embargo, 12 October 1793, "Despatches from U.S. Consuls in Bordeaux," 1; Pléville le Pelley to Talleyrand, 21 October 1797, Corr. Pol., vol. 48.

22. Fulwar Skipwith to James Causten, 30 June, 28 December 1828, Causten-Pickett Papers, vol. 5, Library of Congress, Washington, D.C.; some of the records of the claims are in vols. 9-14, ibid.

23. Bossenger Foster, Jr., to Andrew Craigie, 29 August 1797, Andrew Craigie Papers, vol. 3, American Antiquarian Society, Worcester, Massachusetts.

24. 16 February 1797 in James E. Cronin, ed., *The Diary of Elihu Hubbard Smith* (Philadelphia, 1973), p. 291; Orestus Turner, *History of the Pioneer Settlement of Phelps and Gormans Purchase and Morris Reserve* (Rochester, N.Y. 1851), pp. 50, 335-36; William Blount to James

Mountflorence, 1 November 1791, Dreer Collection, Historical Society of Pennsylvania, Philadelphia, Pennsylvania; Alice B. Keith, ed., "Letters from Major James Cole Mountflorence to Members of the Blount Family," *North Carolina Historical Review* 14 (1937): 254, 264; Shipton, ed., *Biographical Sketches of Those Who Attended Harvard,* 17: 36-44.

25. Hezekiah Pierpont to Fulwar Skipwith, 23 September 1797, Constable Pierpont Papers, vol. 43, New York Public Library, New York, New York.

26. Richard Codman to Sylvanus Bourne, 5 September 1797, 9 March 1798, Bourne Papers, vol. 5, Library of Congress, Washington, D.C.; Mary Pinckney to Margaret Manigault, 23 January 1798, Manigault Family Papers.

27. Editor's Introduction to Michel Missoffe, "Le Prince recoit," in *Talleyrand,* ed., Jacques Lacretelle (Paris, 1964), p. 211.

28. Bizardel, "French Estates, American Landlords," p. 110; Perkins Journal, 17 July 1795.

29. Alexander Baring to John Hope, 8 December 1795 in *William Bingham's Maine Lands,* ed. Frederick Allis, Jr., Colonial Society of Massachusetts *Collections,* vol. 36 (Boston, 1954), pp. 609-11.

30. Durden, "Joel Barlow," pp. 349, 351; Martin Buirst, *At Spes Non Fracta: Hope & Company, 1770-1815* (The Hague, 1974), pp. 368-74.

31. Bizardel, "French Estates, American Landlords," pp. 109-10.

32. Chase C. Mooney, *William H. Crawford* (Lexington, Kentucky, 1974), pp. 58-59.

33. John Marshall to Charles Lee, 3 November 1797, Marshall Papers, Library of Congress, Washington, D.C.; John Trumbull to Jonathan Trumbull, 30 May 1797, John Trumbull Papers, Yale University, New Haven, Connecticut; Irma Jaffe, *John Trumbull* (Boston, 1975). Trumbull claimed that his stock had increased from 2 to 25.

34. Perkins Journal, 1, 4, April 1795.

35. DuPont, *Journey to France and Spain,* p. 41; Bizardel, "French Estates, American Landlords," pp. 111-13; Howard C. Rice, Jr., *Thomas Jefferson's Paris* (Princeton, N.J., 1976), p. 63.

36. John Vanderlyn to Nicholas Vanderlyn, 30 December 1796; quote is from John Vanderlyn to Peter Vanderlyn, 13 July 1798, John Vanderlyn Papers, Senate-House Historical Museum, Kingston, New York; Kenneth C. Lindsay, *The Works of John Vanderlyn* (Binghamton, N.Y., 1970), pp. 127, 128, 151.

37. *Le Moniteur Universel,* 21 February, 29 March, 1798.

38. Mary Pinckney to Margaret Manigault, 23 January 1798, Manigault Family Papers.

39. Ibid.

40. 19 January 1805, in Joyce Hemlow, ed., *The Journal and Letters of Fanny Burney, Madame d'Arblay,* 6 vols. to date (Oxford, 1972), 6: 744, 5: 284n.

41. Gouverneur Morris to John Fenwick, 11, 30 December 1793, "Despatches of U.S. Consuls at Bordeaux," 1, Bizardel, *Américains à Paris,* pp. 72-75.

42. Mary Pinckney to Margaret Manigault, 5 November 1797, Manigault Family Papers; Eugene Müntz, "Les Annexions des Collections d'Art ou de Bibliothèques," *Revue d'Histoire Diplomatique* 9 (1895): 376-78; 10 (1896): 493, 506-7.

43. John C. Greene and John G. Burke, *The Science of Minerals in the Age of Jefferson* (Philadelphia, 1978), p. 99; John F. Fulton and Elizabeth H. Thomson, *Benjamin Silliman: Pathfinder in American Science* (New York, 1968), pp. 87-88.

44. I have relied heavily on Jaffe, *Trumbull.* pp. 172-75; details are in the John Trumbull Letterbook, 1796-1802, New-York Historical Society, New York, New York; Sizer, ed., *Autobiography of Trumbull,* pp. 186-88.

45. Ferdinand Boyer, "Les Responsabilités de Napoléon dans le transfert à Paris des oeuvres d'art de l'étranger, *"Revue d'Histoire Moderne et Contemporarine* 11 (1964): 242, 246; Ferdinand Boyer, "Une Conquête Artistique de la Convention: Les Tableaux de Stathouder (1795), *"Bulletin de la Société de l'Histoire de l'Art Français* (1970): 153-57.

46. Rita S. Gottesman, ed., *The Arts and Crafts in New York: 1799-1804* (New York, 1965), pp. 42-43; Helen W. Henderson, *The Pennsylvania Academy of Fine Arts* (Boston, 1911), pp. 13, 15, 30. William Bentley of Salem noted in his diary, "The Revolution in France has rendered cheap the Clocks, & Pictures of that Nation. And the cheapness has multiplied them in our Country. The decimal division has made them ready to dispose of the old Clocks of 12 hours, & several fine clocks have been an easy purchase to our Seamen. The diposal of so many estates has made pictures also very cheap. Such as have already arrived have been some good pieces, but in general they have ill chosen. Capt. Carnes carried me to see a collection made by his Brother Charles. There were two fine views of Vesuvius & of Aetna, & well Coloured. They exceed the painting of the chamber in Cambridge. The other pieces were fancy & not all of the most chaste character." 15 October 1795, *The Diary of William Bentley,* 4 vols. (Salem, Mass., 1905-1914), 2: 162.

47. Michel M. Swan, *The Athenaeum Gallery* (Boston, 1940), pp. 90-92, 200-82.

48. Howard C. Rice, Jr., "Documents sur le Commerce avec les Neutres en l'an II et III," *Annales Historiques de la Révolution Française* 17 (1940): 177, 179; Rice, "Notes on the Swan Furniture," [Boston] *Bulletin*

of the Museum of Fine Arts 38 (1940): 43, 49; Howard C. Rice, Jr., "A Pair of Sevrés Vases," ibid. 55 (1957): 37; F. J. B. Watson, *The Wrightman Collection*, 2 vols. (Greenwich, 1966), 1: xxii, xxv. Both Clough and Rogers were back in Paris in 1797.

49. Thomas Melville Statement, 20 September 1807, "Despatches from U.S. Consuls in Paris," 1; Robert R. Palmer, "Herman Melville et la Révolution Française," *Annales Historiques de la Révolution Francqise* 26 (1954): 254-56.

50. Ibid.; Raymond Guyot, *Le Directorie et la Paix de l'Europe* (Paris, 1911), pp. 445, 461, 469; Charles Ballot, *Les Négociations de Lille* (Paris, 1910), p. 311.

51. Délibérations, Supplément, Arrestations, 24 August 1797, AF* 3, 156, Archives Nationales, Paris; Registre des Délibérations, 7 July 1797, ibid., p. 153.

52. Joseph E. A. Smith, *The History of Pittsfield* (Boston, Mass., 1876), pp. 398-400.

53. Perkins Journal, 30 March 1795; also 29 February 1796 in *Memoirs of Theobald Wolfe Tone*, ed. William Theobald Tone (London, 1837), p. 256.

54. 6 March 1801 in DuPont, *Journey to France and Spain*, p. 45.

55. Joshua Gilpin Journal, 12, 13, 15, 28 November 1797, 5, 8, 11 January, 4 April 1798, Gilpin Papers.

56. Mary B. Norton, *The British-Americans: The Loyalist Exiles in London: 1774-1789* (Boston, 1972), pp. 62-72.

57. William Lee Diary, 5 March 1796, Lee-Palfrey Papers; Yvon Bizardel, *American Painters in Paris*, trans. Richard Howard (New York, 1960), pp. 63-65.

58. Bizardel, "French Estates, American Landlords," p. 112; Latimer, *Scrap-Book of French Revolution*, p. 67.

59. Fulwar Skipwith to James Causten, 30 June 1828, Causten-Pickett Papers, vol. 5.

60. Thomas Paine, "Letter to George Washington, 30 July 1796" in *The Writings of Thomas Paine*, 2 vols., ed. Philip Foner (New York, 1969), 2: 671-73.

61. Lee Kennett, "John Skey Eustace and the French Revolution," *American Society of Legion of Honor Magazine* 45 (1974): 39.

62. [Boston] *Columbian Centinel*, 17 October 1798.

63. Jaffe, *Trumbull*, p. 207; 25 November 1814 in *The Diary of Harriet Manigault: 1813-1816*, ed. Virginia and James S. Armentrout, Jr. (Philadelphia, 1976), p. 61.

6

"One of the Tryed Patriots of '75"

The envoys began the new year in Paris without having made any noticeable progress in the negotiations. If Pinckney understood his changed status, he made few comments about it except to castigate Gerry. Gerry was invited to Talleyrand's ball, as was Marshall, who declined to go. Marshall and Pinckney refused until late in March to acknowledge that the French were succeeding in dividing the commission irrevocably. The envoys rarely met as a group in their last four months in Paris.

Mary Pinckney noted dangers in their predicament, warning that the envoys must be very careful, because "The temple stares them in the face."[1] Only two weeks before, the papers had carried an announcement of the imprisonment of the Portuguese ambassador Araujo without explanation. In The Hague William Murray inquired of a Dutch emissary to France whether the American envoys were being decisive with the French government, only to be told that the situation of foreign ambassadors in Paris was very delicate.[2] During the envoys' time in Paris four diplomats were sent to the Temple, where leading political prisoners were held. Within the American community only Mary Pinckney spoke openly of this danger, but certainly the envoys understood what might happen if the Directory stripped them of their diplomatic status.

In January Caron de Beaumarchais entered the negotiations. Beaumarchais did not break his relations with Pinckney but simply made them social. To Marshall and Gerry, conveniently residing at his friend Madame de Villette's apartments, Beaumarchais submitted a paper, approved by Talleyrand and Bellamy. In this paper Beaumarchais argued that President Adams had been belligerent toward France in his speech of 16 May 1797. He then went on to criticize Adams's statements at the opening of the regular session of Congress in November. Beaumarchais's arguments were more sophisticated than those of Bellamy and Hottinguer, containing a modicum of validity, but the demands were the same except for the omission of the payment of a bribe. Gerry and Marshall discussed the paper without consulting Pinckney.[3] Neither envoy was ready to retreat, however, and they refused to apologize or explain Adams's position toward France.

Louis d'Autremont, whose name appears as Dutrimont in the dispatches, then entered the negotiations, holding frequent conferences with Gerry. Having returned to Europe in 1796 with Talleyrand, d'Autremont now served as one of the foreign minister's private secretaries in addition to selling American lands.[4] D'Autremont made it clear that he spoke for Talleyrand, while Beaumarchais insisted that he acted only as a longtime friend of the American cause.

At this time Pierre DuPont de Nemours began to call on Pinckney more frequently. The elder DuPont would explain that he intended to migrate to the United States, which he would shortly do, and wanted information on land purchases. DuPont knew that the foreign office had tried to exclude Pinckney but kept this information from him. Instead, DuPont himself apparently believed that specious explanation that Pinckney's exclusion developed from a confusion between Charles and his brother, Thomas Pinckney, former minister to Great Britain. He claimed that he had been unable to convince the foreign office of its error.[5] DuPont was an effective intermediary to Pinckney, because he himself was gullible in accepting the arguments that Talleyrand's associates presented. DuPont's role at this point was to determine whether or not Pinckney was going to force a break in the negotiations.

The only tangible public results in the final three months of the negotiations were memorials—manifestos might be a better word —and countermemorials. These documents served the interests of posterity rather than diplomacy, as each side justified a more rigid position that any it had taken since October. The envoys sent

Talleyrand a lengthy statement of the American position at the end of January, written mainly by Marshall and extravagantly described by his biographer Albert Beveridge as "one of the ablest state papers produced by American diplomacy."[6]

In this paper Marshall reiterated American grievances based on the doctrine of neutrality as Jefferson had enunciated it to the British in 1793. Talleyrand made no response and told Henry Rutledge, who was sent to ask whether the Americans could expect a reply, that the French were not accustomed to receiving such long epistles. The foreign office had carefully read the document, but offered no indication to the Americans that an answer would be forthcoming quickly.[7] After waiting three more weeks, Marshall pressed Gerry to request their passports. Gerry agreed, but matters of state were postponed while Marshall and Gerry escorted Madame de Villette and another Frenchwoman on a long weekend to Madame de Villette's country chateau. Gerry offered to forgo the weekend in the country, but Marshall accepted this diversion with pleasure.[8]

Talleyrand devised new tactics to counter the demands made in the American memorial. He won approval of a loan, which he had not done in his first memoir in October, and he insisted that the Americans be required to offer an explanation of Adams's speech. The strategy of delay was thus to continue. Now, however, Talleyrand proposed to negotiate only with the most receptive envoys and send the other two away.[9] Since Talleyrand waited for another month before giving the document to the envoys, he was probably still undecided as to whether Marshall or Gerry would be most receptive to French demands.

Between the time the Directory approved Talleyrand's new plan and his release of the document, the French government gave strong hints to the American community that war might be in the offing if negotiations broke down. Furthermore, two of the envoys had not shown any friendship to France. Immediately a barrage of letters was sent back to the United States assailing the commission, its composition, and its bellicose attitude. The letters display a striking uniformity, even without any guidance by the French government. The leaders of the American community were willing, as

Mary Pinckney had pointed out, to castigate their own countrymen while explaining away French mistakes and imperialism. The *Aurora* quoted a letter from Paris calling Marshall "an unequivocal enemy of France" and concluding that Adams "should have sent a Republican and not such a man as Mr. Marshall."[10]

Nathaniel Cutting said that he pitied Gerry's mortifying situation, but that was just part of the problem. "The cold reception, bordering on contempt, which the *Extraordinary Envoys* have met with from the Directorie of France is the most striking comment that can be given on the imbecile and supercilious conduct of many conspicuous characters *in the government* of the United States."[11] Fulwar Skipwith maintained that Marshall and Pinckney did not attempt to conceal "that the doors are open only to the intriguants against the enemies of the present Government." He claimed that "the name of a true supporter of the french revolution is as grating to their ears as his sight is to their eyes." In his explanation to Jefferson, Skipwith revealed how little he knew about Talleyrand's policy, noting that "their closest counsellor seems to be Beaumarchais."[12]

Joel Barlow contributed to the attack on the envoys.

The first [Pinckney] was a man who had just been refused & could not be offered again without an insult, as it was so received. The second [Marshall] was a man whose effegy had been burnt in Virginia for his violent defense of the English treaty, at least it was so reported & believed in this place, the third [Gerry] was a little make-weight man appointed with the intention that he should not have influence. . . .if Gerry had been sent alone, and not been shackled with the other two, the Directorie would have negotiated with him without any difficulty.[13]

Like other Americans in Paris, Skipwith respected Gerry, whom he called "one of the tryed patriots of '75 and one of the remaining republican chiefs of the American states," but he doubted Gerry's ability to stand up to the other envoys and take decisive action alone. At this time, however, most members of the American community in Paris did not see any essential differences among the three envoys, except that Gerry seemed basically more sympathetic to the French cause. Gerry had not associated closely with Americans in Paris, and probably Talleyrand had not yet chosen him as the point from which to disrupt the commission.

Skipwith went further than most Americans in Paris by urging a policy that all envoys rejected. He believed that the time had come for the United States to "confess some of our errors" and "lay their sins heavily upon the shoulders of a few persons who perpetrated them,"meaning the Federalists, of course. The United States, he said, must "modify or break the English treaty with Jay, and to lend France as much money, should she ask for it, as she lent us in our hour of distress."[15] Not only did Americans in Paris fail to grasp the deeper problems of the negotiations, but they also willingly interjected themselves into a bitter partisan conflict in the United States. It was not the French but the American residents of Paris who boldly intervened in American diplomacy and politics.

In the last week of February Gerry and Marshall returned from their visit to the country to find a different situation, at least in Gerry's eyes. After meeting with d'Autremont on the day of his return, Gerry reported that Talleyrand now sought a loan to be granted at the end of the war with Great Britain, an arrangement thus preserving the facade of American neutrality. Gerry argued that this represented a change in the French position. Since their instructions only forbade a loan during the war, he argued, the envoys had the power to consider the new proposal. Marshall and Pinckney violently disagreed, thereby breaking the fragile relationship that had united the three envoys. Talleyrand's new proposal was only a tactic, Marshall and Pinckney declared, to keep the envoys in Paris while the French continued the war against American commerce. Compromising their private positions, the envoys asked for their first meeting with Talleyrand since October. They agreed that Pinckney, as nominal head of the commission, would not reveal to Talleyrand that their instructions positively forbade any loan to France, unless he believed it absolutely necessary.[16]

In the first week of March the envoys met twice with Talleyrand, for the first time discussing substantive issues. Rather than serving to open formal talks, these meetings convinced each side that an impasse had been reached. First, Talleyrand resorted to the tactic of putting the Americans on the defensive. He asked for an explanation of certain passages in Washington's Farewell Address. Pinckney observed that this was a new complaint, but Talleyrand then dropped the matter by declaring that Washington's speech had wounded the Directory. Probing the envoys to determine whether they had received new instructions, Talleyrand was disappointed that the envoys had not, nor had they asked for any, particularly on the question of a loan. During their second meeting, Pinckney announced that the envoys had been forbidden to agree to a loan of any kind. Although the Americans thought they detected a look of surprise on Talleyrand's face, he had received the same information from Pitcairn after Pitcairn had talked with Pinckney in November.[17] More important for Adams's later decisions, Talleyrand now dropped the demand for a loan. The envoys made clear to the foreign minister that they would not consider any explanation of Washington's or Adams's speeches, and Talleyrand subsequently dropped this demand as well.

The maneuvers by each side to cast blame on the other for the impending collapse of the negotiations obscured what had been accomplished. Talleyrand still made no offer to stop French maritime abuses or discrimination against American vessels. The envoys refused to acknowledge any contradiction between Jay's Treaty and the French Alliance. Although they had not been officially received, the envoys now met with the foreign minister rather than his unaccredited agents—a significant change. Furthermore, the bribe ultimata had not been renewed. Each side had had to assess the other's position and determination. The negotiations were deadlocked but not hopelessly so.

As a result of his meetings with the envoys, Talleyrand released his February memorial and arranged to have it sent to the United States for translation and publication in American newspapers. He insisted that one American who was "impartial" stay in Paris and negotiate.[18] The meetings with Marshall had convinced Talleyrand that he had grown as obstinate as Pinckney. Rather than accepting the invitation to depart, however, Marshall and Pinckney set to work on an answer to Talleyrand. They, too, took special care to see that copies of their memorial reached the United States quickly.[19] It was almost as if the negotiations were being conducted by newspapers three thousand miles from Paris.

Publication of charges and countercharges became the mode of French-American diplomacy in the first half of 1798. Within a day of the submission of the envoys' April memorial to Talleyrand, Congress ordered publication of their first dispatches, thus touching off the XYZ affair in the United States. Gerry had reported Bellamy's statement

that it was worthy of the attention of the Envoys to consider whether by so small a sacrifice [a loan] they would establish a peace with France, or whether they would risk the consequences; that if nothing could be done by the envoys, arrangements could be made forthwith to ravage the coasts of the United States by frigates from Santo Domingo; that small States which had offended France were suffering by it; that Hamburg and other Cities in that quarter would within a month or two have their Government changed; that Switzerland would undergo the same operation; and Portugal would probably be in a worse predicament; that the expedition against England would be certainly pursued; and that the present period was the most favorable, if we wished to adopt any measures for pacification. [20]

Gerry also quoted Talleyrand to the effect "that the information Mr. Bellamy had given me was just and might always be relied on." No amount of argument by Talleyrand or by a few Americans in Paris could begin to counteract the revulsion caused by these revelations. Talleyrand's report, which was published in June, discussed consuls' rights, prize courts, and American violations of treaties, while his agents spoke of crushing the United States if that nation did not submit to France. [21]

In Paris, Gerry informed his colleagues that he would remain there if his presence would prevent war. [22] Marshall and Pinckney had little doubt that Gerry had long since made his decision. In early April they prepared to depart without demanding their passports or being officially asked to leave. The situation produced no expulsions or ultimata but rather a tacit acknowledgement that Gerry would remain. Gerry complained to John Adams that he now found himself virtually a hostage, sacrificing his reputation to the hope for peace with France. [23] The other two envoys left Paris with animus toward Gerry. Mary Pinckney charged that he "had been false to his colleagues and wanting to his country." [24]

But Talleyrand's hope that he would have an "impartial" Gerry with whom to deal was quickly dispelled. From the beginning of the mission Gerry had seen the United States as right and France as wrong in the dispute, but he considered the prevention of war as paramount. Gerry informed Talleyrand that he could not negotiate officially and that France had no right to choose which American would represent the United States. He further explained that he would remain only long enough to receive instructions from Adams, which he hoped would assure the continuation of diplomatic relations. Nonetheless, in July, Talleyrand informed Directory that the best way to prevent war was to keep Gerry in Paris as long as possible.[25]

Gerry's decision to remain in Paris has been described by his most recent biographer as "right though for the wrong reasons."[26] Gerry did not altogether disagree with Marshall's conclusion that France would not declare war on the United States, but he was not willing to risk the possibility that they were mistaken. Gerry's continued presence in Paris allowed Talleyrand to maintain that negotiations were proceeding and no rupture with the United States had occurred. In the United States, Adams did not openly repudiate Gerry, and thus the extreme Federalists had to postpone consideration of a declaration of war until Gerry's return in October, when some of the domestic passions over the XYZ affair had subsided.

Between April and August 1798, Gerry achieved limited progress. The prohibition of American ships in French ports was modifed. In a sweeping order the government ordered a cessation of maritime attacks. It has been said that Talleyrand took this action after reading Victor DuPont's highly critical attack on French policy following his return from the United States in the summer of 1798.[27] But Talleyrand himself had advocated the same policy the previous October, so the DuPont memoir simply offered a justification for implementing the policy. DuPont had asserted, however, that if French maritime policy were continued, the United States might go to war, which Talleyrand had not believed earlier. To avoid war had been the goal of Talleyrand's erratic diplomacy, and the time for an open concession demonstrating French good intentions had come. Gerry redeemed a small amount of his reputation by being

Figure 10. Portrait of Elbridge Gerry, 1798, by John Vanderlyn. *Courtesy of the Fogg Art Museum, Harvard University. Purchase-Louise E. Bettens Fund.*

able to claim credit for this policy change, although whether his remaining in Paris caused it is doubtful.

After the departure of his colleagues, Gerry worked closely with Barlow, Codman, and Skipwith, who became the unofficial agents of the American government. In a meeting with Talleyrand, Codman found the foreign minister much more receptive to American arguments than before. After discussing this conference with Gerry, Codman wrote his highly influential letter to Harrison Otis advocating the appointment of a new commission and outlining French concessions.[28] Acting at Gerry's suggestion, Barlow met with Victor DuPont on his return to France to discuss American intentions that may have influenced his memoir to Talleyrand.[29] Writing one of his old business partners, Barlow disclosed that the French would not demand a loan—his first acknowledgment that he knew of such a demand—and urged that a second commission be appointed.[30] Skipwith, who continued to hold the title of consul although he had resigned in 1796, met with Talleyrand several times. The foreign minister indicated that he would officially announce that any new American envoys would be received, a direct response to Adams's demand for assurances on this point. Skipwith talked to Talleyrand and de laForest about who the prospective envoys might be and observed that William Short might present problems because of known anti-revolutionary pronouncements.[31] To a greater degree than Gerry, these members of the American community in Paris worked out the details for future negotiations, if there were to be any, between the two countries.

By mid-May, published copies of the envoys' dispatches had reached Great Britain, where they were quickly reprinted by the British and distributed throughout Europe. The dispatches carried the initials W, X, Y, and Z, which Pickering had inserted for Hubbard, Hottinguer, Bellamy, and Hauteval. In Philadelphia it had been assumed that the envoys would have left Paris by the time the dispatches reached Europe, but Gerry and Pinckney both remained in France. They complained that Congress had needlessly endangered them by this rash act.[32] The publication of the dispatches revealed that Gerry had agreed with his colleagues to a greater extent than either Talleyrand or members of the American community suspected.

Sandoz Rollin, the Prussian ambassador and Talleyrand's confidant, called on the foreign minister the day the XYZ dispatches were published in Paris. From Talleyrand's comments he deduced that the charges of bribery were certainly true. Talleyrand charged that the American government was trying to force him out of office.[33] In reality, the publication of the dispatches merely prevented Talleyrand from resigning his office to assume the ambassadorship to Constantinople, a step he had planned in conjunction with Napoleon's Egyptian campaign.[34]

Talleyrand did not need to fear for his position. While the war with England continued, the Directory saw little need for immediate peace with the United States. In contrast to Talleyrand, a majority of the Directory remained adamant on the question of an apology for the Jay Treaty. The release of the dispatches could not force Talleyrand's resignation unless other policy considerations came into play. The foreign minister had secured Napoleon's support, and no attempt was made to replace him, despite growing attacks in the newspapers.

Within a month after the dispatches arrived, Talleyrand had regained control of American policy.[35] He did so by issuing a public denunciation of the unofficial agents who had misled the American envoys. He insisted that Gerry reveal to him the identities of W, X, Y, and Z. In a move that drew bitter criticism in the United States, Gerry accepted Talleyrand's appeal and confidentially revealed the names. Actually, Gerry grasped the situation better than his numerous critics in the United States.[36] Talleyrand then denounced these men as unofficial agents who at no time acted in his name, thus repudiating all overtures and demands made during the first few months that the envoys had been in Paris. This renunciation included the bribery and loan demands. Hauteval and Bellamy publicly identified themselves, and in the safety of Hamburg Bellamy contradicted Talleyrand's disavowal of him.[37]

In June and July Talleyrand grew alarmed at reports that the United States was preparing for war. For the first time, war with the United States seemed a possibility for Frenchmen and a probability for officials in the foreign ministry. Congress had unilaterally canceled the French-American alliance, made provisions to raise an army, sent ships against French forces in the West Indies, and passed the alien laws that expelled many French émigrés in the United States. Unquestionably the United States was moving closer to Great Britain; yet the underlying aim of French policy toward the United States was to prevent this. In quick order, the Directory and Talleyrand reversed themselves, eliminating all commissions to privateers, relaxing embargoes against American ships in French ports, dropping the demand for a *role d'équipage*, and releasing American seamen from jails.

Gerry deserved a degree of credit for remaining in Paris to witness and participate in the welcome changes in French policy. Americans in Paris bombarded their friends at home with reports of the changing situation. When first learning of the United States' hostile measures, Mark Leavenworth, the largest American specu-lator in French inscriptions and a man whose holdings amounted to over 15 million francs, considered war inevitable. Four days later he learned that Gerry was to stay in Paris and renewed his faltering hope that progress was being made. He concluded, however, that it was "perhaps difficult to say which side had conducted [itself] most stupidly."[38] John Vanderlyn did not regret that Gerry "stays so long for it may probably have a good effect."[39] Richard Codman believed that "the moment is extremely favorable for an accom-modation, I hope most sincerely that our govt. will see it in the same Light and once more risque sending a minister."[40] From Talley-rand, Gerry received assurances that the United States could send a new minister, and the French government would officially receive him, regardless of his political inclinations.

When Marshall arrived in the United States in mid-June, he was fêted as a symbol of the staunch American renouncing Europe's corruptions. Not a little of this outpouring reflected Federalist ef-forts to secure the political advantage they had just gained through the XYZ exposé. Marshall, however, was not the man the extreme Federalists in Adams's cabinet wanted at that moment. He argued, as he had for six months in Paris, that France did not want war and would not declare it. He believed that if the defensive measures Adams had proposed in May 1797 had been adopted, they would have been "the best negotiator we could have employed."[41]

Americans argued over the meaning of Marshall's statements and French intentions. Federalist Roger Griswold, who had earlier described a possible war with France as a battle of "order and Government against disorder and Jacobinism," said after Marshall's return that "all parties appear to agree in the certainty of war." Benjamin Franklin Bache, editor of the *Aurora*, wrote privately that "war is inevitable between my country and France, our govern-ment has truly lost its head." But both of these opinions fell at opposite ends of the political spectrum.[42]

The confusion over the administration's exact goals was understandable. Publicly Adams denounced France and appeared increasingly belligerent in his statements in response to petitions supporting his policy. Privately he started to maintain his own counsel much more than he had in his first year in office. But he never closed the door to future negotiations with France after the publication of the dispatches or following Marshall's return. At the time of Marshall's arrival in Philadelphia Adams announced that he would not send any representatives to France unless he received acknowledgment beforehand that they would be officially received. Gerry's letter to Adams defending his decision to stay in Paris to prevent war between the two republics was printed.[43] War was definitely in the air, but at the same time other indications suggested that Adams might still seek a peaceful resolution of the issues.

Now completely excluded from all discussions concerning France, Thomas Jefferson vacillated between hopes for peace and fears that the Federalists would incite war. Before the publication of the dispatches he believed that the "best anchor of our hope is an invasion of England, if they republicanize that country, all will be safe with us," but after the revelations Jefferson found not "one motive the more for going to war." Jefferson correctly saw that Marshall "is much cooler than his friends wish" about the prospects for war.[44]

In the summer of 1798 the XYZ affair had its most profound consequences in eliminating Republican opposition to Adams's foreign policy. In Virginia Republican representatives met after the publication of the dispatches and decided not to resist Adams's defensive proposals, which passed quickly along with the Alien and Sedition Acts.[45] Disputes among Federalists had more significance than conflicts between parties. But few perceived this development at the time when Adams announced the dispatch of a second mission in early 1799. In the intervening months the country was rocked with bitter and sometimes violent disputes and intrigues.

Those responsible for implementing policy toward France became the objects of controversy. In March Samuel M. Hopkins and William Lee left Paris with dispatches containing information on the envoys' meetings with Talleyrand in the first week of the month. They also carried letters from Talleyrand to a number of people in

Philadelphia, including Moreau St. Méry.[46] A letter to Benjamin Bache included Talleyrand's memoir on French-American relations, which he had submitted to the envoys just as Hopkins and Lee were leaving Paris.[47]

Bache received the memoir and published it a few days before the government had officially received it. Bache was then accused of private correspondence with Talleyrand and held in contempt of Congress, which marked the start of a persecution of Republican newspaper editors that reached its peak under the Sedition Acts. Bache explained how he received the dispatch and from whom, but to no avail.[48] The French had threatened to defeat the Federalists by fomenting support for the opposition, and Bache's action seemed to confirm these tactics. One observer in Philadelphia reported that crowds of young men had awakened Adams and praised him, then proceeded to Bache's *Aurora* offices and vandalized his printing shop.[49]

William Lee, who sought a consulship in France, and Hopkins became alarmed that their reputations would be tarnished by disloyalty, simply for having carried the dispatches and Talleyrand's letters. They declined to carry the dispatches from New York on to Philadelphia, thus leaving the unwelcome task to John Kidder. Oliver Wolcott, Jr., who had become an expert in detecting Republican intrigues after his involvement in Edmund Randolph's resignation, cross-examined Lee and Hopkins about the letters and packets that they had carried from France. Wolcott ignored Marshall's return to Philadelphia, which would have offered him a source for more current information, since Marshall had left France a month after Hopkins and Lee. Instead, he preferred to attack the integrity and loyalty of Republicans, an approach characteristic of Adams's cabinet in the summer of 1798. Wolcott repeatedly asked Lee and Hopkins if Talleyrand had sent any letters to Jefferson, only to learn that there were none. Unwilling to return to Philadelphia without news of his Republican enemy, Wolcott then copied the letters that Cutting, Barlow, and Skipwith had written to Jefferson.[50]

Adams did not escape the upheavals caused by his erratic French policy, even though Congress enacted his legislative program. After Congress adjourned without declaring war, Adams stopped in New York en route to Braintree. Word spread that Adams planned to attend the theater that evening, and a large crowd gathered in anticipation. One observer assumed that the crowd assembled to honor the president.[51] Another diarist at the same event reported that a member of the crowd assaulted Adams's secretary after he identified himself.[52] The president himself remained with friends for the evening.

Any connection with French policy, whether in implementing it or opposing it, might cause suspicion or even violence, as John Marshall discovered as he returned to Richmond from Philadelphia. After receiving a warm welcome in Federalist areas such as Lancaster, Pennsylvania, Marshall's appearance at the theater in Fredericksburg caused a riot between Republicans and Federalists.[53] Frustration over French policy seemed to cause Americans to direct their energies to the messengers rather than the message in the summer of 1798.

The XYZ affair did not end until the Senate ratified the Convention of Mortefontaine in the last months of Adams's term, but the tensions caused by the possibility of war began to dissipate soon after Adams arrived at Braintree. Gerry landed in October, immediately leaving shipboard to visit Adams, even before seeing his family. Gerry convinced his old friend that France did not want, and would not declare, war. By this time Adams knew that all three envoys agreed on this fundamental point. In the fall of 1798, Federalists and Republicans waited for the president's decision. Adams's unilateral decision to appoint a new commission to France reflected Gerry's continuing influence, although he had also received the same recommendations from John Q. Adams, William V. Murray, Joel Barlow, and George Logan.[54] The appointment of a second commission to France in February 1799, Adams knew, was the best way to preserve the cherished policy of neutrality.

Adams had first tried to deal with the French problem as he and Jefferson walked the streets of Philadelphia in March 1797. Given the risks and uncertainty of the situation in 1798, it is not surprising that Adams supported and trusted Gerry, the one man among his cabinet members and envoys who had stood with him in 1775 and 1776. When Adams had to reach difficult decisions, he turned to those men who had shared his experience of the American Revolution. He always believed that this period tested and shaped men's characters more than did later political battles between Republicans and Federalists under the Constitution. This conviction was a point lost on high Federalists, to whom the current political alignment was all-important. But for Adams, the American Revolution was the pivotal point of his life, both intellectually and emotionally. This experience thrust him into national politics and accepting counsel from any other source in reaching his final decision to put the XYZ affair behind and begin anew his search for peace with France would not have been characteristic of him.

Notes

1. Mary Pinckney to Margaret Manigault, 23 January 1798, Manigault Family Papers, University of South Carolina, Columbia, South Carolina.

2. *Le Moniteur Universel*, 4 January 1798, 7 April 1798, William V. Murray Common Place Book, vol. 2, Murray Papers, Library of Congress, Washington, D.C.

3. Notations on two drafts of Caron de Beaumarchais to Elbridge Gerry and John Marshall, 13, 15 January 1798; Gerry to Beaumarchais, 15 January 1798, Private Archives, Paris; Beaumarchais to Gerry and Marshall, 17 January 1798, Gerry Papers, Pierpont Morgan Library, New York, New York.

4. John Marshall Journal, 3 February 1798 in Pickering Papers, Massachusetts Historical Society, Boston, Massachusetts; on the identification of d'Autremont, see William Rawle to Timothy Pickering, 31 October 1798, Pickering Papers; on the family in Asylum, see Theophile Cazenove's report on the Asylum Company, Holland Land Company Papers, vol. 268, Gemeentearchief, Amsterdam; passport list in F 7, 642, Archives Nationales, Paris.

5. Mack Thompson, "Causes and Circumstances of the DuPont Family's Emigration," *French Historical Studies* 6 (1969): 66-68, 70; Pierre DuPont de Nemours to Victor Dupont, 2 January 1798, DuPont Family Papers, Eleutherian Mills Historical Library, Wilmington, Delaware.

6. Albert Beveridge, *The Life of John Marshall*, 4 vols. (Boston, 1916-1919), 2: 297; American Envoys to Talleyrand, 31 January 1798, Correspondance Politique, États-Unis, vol. 49, Archives du Ministère des Affaires Étrangères, Paris (hereafter, Corr. Pol.).

7. Ibid.; American Envoys to Timothy Pickering, 7 February 1798, "Diplomatic Despatches France," 6, Record Group 59, National Archives, Washington, D.C.

8. Mary Pinckney to Margaret Manigault, 9 March 1798, Manigault Family Papers; Charles C. Pinckney to Thomas Pinckney, 13 March 1798,

Free Library of Philadelphia, Philadelphia, Pennsylvania; John Marshall to [Charles Lee], 4 March 1798, ibid.; American Envoys to Nathaniel Cutting, 27 February 1798, Gerry Papers, Henry E. Huntington Library, San Marino, California; Elbridge Gerry to John Adams, 8 July 1799, Gerry Papers, Library of Congress. Washington, D.C.

9. Tallyrand, Memoir, [3-18] February 1798, Corr. Pol., vol 49.

10. *Aurora*, 20 March 1798.

11. Nathaniel Cutting to James Monroe, 22 February 1798. Nathaniel Cutting Papers, Massachusetts Historical Society, Boston, Massachusetts, italics in original.

12. Fulwar Skipwith to Thomas Jefferson, 17 March 1798, Wolcott Papers, vol. 12, Connecticut Historical Society, Hartford, Connecticut. It is unclear whether Jefferson received the original of this letter.

13. Joel Barlow to Abraham Baldwin. 4 March 1798, Barlow Papers, vol. 4, Harvard University, Cambridge, Massachusetts.

14. Fulwar Skipwith to Thomas Jefferson, 17 March 1798, Wolcott Papers, vol. 12.

15. Ibid.

16. Memorandum to American Envoys [5 March 1798], Pinckney Family Papers, Library of Congress; American Envoys to Timothy Pickering, 9 March 1798, "Diplomatic Despatches, France," 6, Record Group 59.

17. Ibid.

18. Talleyrand to American Envoys, 18 March 1798, Gerry Papers, Pierpont Morgan Library; copy with margin notations ordering translation in Corr. Pol., vol. 49.

19. American Envoys to Talleyrand, 3 April 1798, Corr. Pol., vol. 49. copy in American Envoys to Timothy Pickering, 3 April 1798. "Diplomatic Despatches, France," 6, Record Group 59.

20. Quote is from American Envoys to Timothy Pickering, 24 December 1797, ibid.; in *Message of the President of the United States submitted to both Houses of Congress, April 3, 1798* (Philadelphia 1798), p. 67, Pickering subsituted Y for Bellamy.

21. *Aurora*, 15, 16 June 1798.

22. Marshall Journal, [19]-20 March 1798.

23. John Marshall to Talleyrand, 13 April 1798, Corr. Pol., vol. 49; Talleyrand to Pinckney and Marshall, 13 April 1798, ibid.; Elbridge Gerry to John Adams, 16 April 1798, Adams Family Papers, Massachusetts Historical Society, Boston, Massachusetts.

24. Mary Pinckney to Margaret Manigault, 15 April 1798, Manigault Family Papers.

25. Elbridge Gerry to Talleyrand, 20 April 1798, Pickering Papers; Talleyrand to Directory, 10 July 1798, Corr. Pol., vol. 50; the best account

of Gerry in Paris after the other envoys' departure is George Billias, *Elbridge Gerry* (New York, 1976), pp. 254-86.

26. Ibid., p. 265.

27. Samuel E. Morison, "DuPont, Talleyrand, and the French Spoliations," Massachusetts Historical Society, *Proceedings* 69 (1915-1916): 64; Morrison reprints the DuPont Memorandum in ibid. pp. 65-76.

28. Richard Codman, "Conversations with Talleyrand," 3 July 1798, Gerry Papers, Pierpont Morgan Library; Codman to Harrison G. Otis, 26 August 1798, "Misc. Letters," M-179, Record Group 59, National Archives.

29. Elbridge Gerry to Victor DuPont, 23 June 1798, DuPont Family Papers.

30. Joel Barlow to James Watson, 26 July 1798, Barlow Papers, vol. 4, Harvard University, Cambridge, Massachusetts; Barlow to Samuel M. Hopkins, 17 July 1798, Beinecke Library, Yale University, New Haven, Connecticut.

31. Fulwar Skipwith to Elbridge Gerry, 6 August 1798, Gerry Papers, Pierpont Morgan Library.

32. Mary Pinckney to Margaret Manigault, 28 May 1798, Manigault Family Papers; Elbridge Gerry to John Adams, 8 July 1799, Adams Papers.

33. Sandoz Rollin dispatch, 31 May 1798, in *Preussen und Frankreich von 1795 bis 1807: Diplomatische Correspondenzen*, ed. Paul Bailleu, 2 vols. (Leipzig, 1881-1887), 1: 210 (hereafter, Dip. Corr.).

34. Carl Lokke, "Pourquoi Talleyrand ne fut pas Envoyé à Constantinople," *Annales Historiques de la Révolution Française*, 11(1933): 157-58.

35. Sandoz Rollin dispatch, 28 June 1798, *Dip. Corr.*. 1: 213.

36. Billias, *Gerry*, p. 284.

37. Hauteval and Bellamy's statements were printed in France and the United States; they are in Corr. Pol., États-Unis, Supplement, vol. 2, 25 June 1798, for Bellamy; Lucien Hauteval to Talleyrand, 1 June 1798, ibid; also Hauteval to John Adams, 26 August 1798, Adams Papers.

38. On Leavenworth's wealth, see Oliver Phelps, Jr., to Oliver Phelps, 1 May 1797, Phelps and Gorham Papers, Box 10, New York State Library, Albany, N.Y.; Mark Leavenworth to Oliver Phelps, Jr., 19 July 1798, ibid., Box 84.

39. John Vanderlyn to Peter Vanderlyn, 13 July 1798, John Vanderlyn Papers, Senate and House Museum, Kingston, New York.

40. Richard Codman to Harrison Otis, 26 August 1798, "Misc. Letters," Record Group 59.

41. Abigail Adams to Jeremy Belknap, 21 June 1798, Adams Papers.

42. Roger Griswold to Fanny Griswold, 29 May, 28 June 1798, Griswold Papers, Yale University, New Haven, Connecticut; Benjamin F.

Bache to Louis G. Cramer, 27 June 1798, Lucien Cramer, ed., *Une famille genevoise, Les Cramers* (Geneva, 1952), pp. 70-71.

43. 21 June 1798, *Annals*, 5th Cong., 9: 3459-60.

44. Quotes from Thomas Jefferson to Thomas Randolph, 11 January 1798, Thomas Jefferson Papers, Library of Congress, Washington, D.C.; Jefferson to Peter Carr, 12 April 1798, ibid; Jefferson to Thomas Randolph, 21 June 1798, ibid; also Jefferson to James Madison, 21 June 1798, James Madison Papers, Library of Congress, Washington, D.C.

45. LeRoy, Bayard, & McEvers to P. & C. Van Eeghen, 12 April 1798, Holland Land Company Papers, vol. 153.

46. Talleyrand to Moreau St. Méry, 28 March 1798, received 21 June 1798 in Moreau de Saint Méry, *Voyage aux États-Unis de l'Amerique, 1793-1798*, ed. Stewart L. Mims (New Haven, Conn. 1913), pp. 260-61.

47. Printed in *Aurora*, 16 June 1798.

48. *Aurora*, 21, 23, 25 June 1798; Bache also printed the commissioner's answer to Talleyrand, ibid., 20 June 1798.

49. 6 May 1798 in Julian U. Niemcewicz, *Under Their Vine and Fig Tree*, ed. and trans. Metchie J. C. Budka (Elizabeth, N.J., 1965), pp. 67-68.

50. 20 June 1798 in *Diary of William Dunlap*, 4 vols. ed. Dorothy C. Barck, New-York Historical Society *Collections* (New York, 1929), 1: 294.

51. 27 July 1798 in *The Diary of Elihu Hubbard Smith*. ed. James E. Cronin (Philadelphia, 1973), p. 458.

52. 28 July 1798 in *Diary of W. Dunlap*. 1: 318.

53. For various accounts, see [Richmond] *Virginia Gazette and General Advertiser*, 14 August 1798; *Alexandria Gazette*; 9 August 1798: *Aurora*, 20 August 1798.

54. John Adams Letters to the *Boston Patriot* in *The Works of John Adams*, 10 vols., ed. Charles F. Adams (Boston, 1854), 9: 241, 244-46; Stephen G. Kurtz, "The French Mission of 1799-1800: Concluding Chapter in the Statecraft of John Adams," *Political Science Quarterly* 80 (1965), pp. 543-57.

7

"In America Only"

After his defeat in the presidential election of 1800, John Adams claimed that his decision to negotiate with France had saved the country from war. At the same time, he believed, this act had cost him his reelection. In these comments, Adams demonstrated two of his least attractive traits. One was that he frequently evoked self-pity in seeking recognition for what he considered truly noble, disinterested acts. Secondly, we see his tendency to try to rewrite American history from his own narrow point of view. In this instance, however, Adams was at least partly right. Acting on his own instincts and principles, Adams prevented the United States from entering a needless war. For this he rightfully deserved the credit he wanted, and certainly in this respect alone his record as president must be judged as superior to that of many others.

But perhaps the real question is this: given the hysteria that developed over the XYZ affair, how did the United States avoid war with France?[1] Adams has claimed too much responsibility for himself alone. He correctly stated that he did have a more consistent policy toward France between 1797 and 1801 than Republicans or even many members of his own party acknowledged. Adams did not want war with France. As president he strongly believed in continuing Washington's policy of neutrality, and never did he ask Congress for a declaration of war. He did write two different drafts of a speech asking for war with France, but he never seems to have conferred with any members of his cabinet on this question.[2]

In his interpretation of events, however, Adams forgot that Talleyrand did not expect war with the United States. After he became convinced that Congress seriously intended to prepare for war, Talleyrand belatedly sought compromise. We do not know whether Talleyrand, even if he so desired, would have been able to convince the Directory in 1798 or, more important, Napoleon after 1799 to declare war on the United States. Following the post-ponement in 1798 of the invasion of Great Britain, the entire question of raiding American commerce appeared in a different light. If privateering continued, it would drive the United States more firmly into British hands as it had already started to do.[3] Thus Talleyrand moved to restrict abuses against American commerce and seamen and made it clear that he would welcome new negotiations.

Indisputably, a significant anti-French fervor swept the United States in 1798 as a result of the XYZ affair. This is not quite the same as saying that a majority of American leaders were willing to go to war. Many Federalists supported Adams's renewed attempt for peace in 1799, as did almost all Republicans. Although individual Federalists differed with Adams as to the exact approach to use, among those leaders who approved the second mission to France were Washington, Hamilton, Pinckney, Marshall, Gerry, Murray, John Q. Adams, Charles Lee, and Henry Knox. Extremists such as Roger Griswold, Rufus King, Timothy Pickering, George Cabot, and James McHenry did not represent or influence Adams's thinking about French policy at this time in his administration.

One scholar has argued that the XYZ affair gave the Federalists solid political advantages and that war with France would probably have had popular support.[4] The evidence is quite inconclusive, because it is difficult to determine whether the Federalists' anti-French pronouncements indicated a real desire for war. There is, to be sure, limited evidence in the Maryland and Virginia elections of 1798 and 1799 that the Federalists were able to capitalize on the issue. John Marshall's election in 1799 is not as clear an indication of the effects of the XYZ affair as has often been alleged, however. Marshall ran from the Richmond district, which was among the Federalist strongholds in Virginia. He had distinguished himself among lawyers and had achieved a solid local reputation before he served as an American envoy. During the campaign French policy and the XYZ affair were discussed in detail, but Marshall persisted in his statements that he did not believe either that France wanted war or that the United States should go to war with France. His opponent, John Clopton, retreated from his own previous attacks on Adams and his generally pro-French position. As one candidate ideally suited to exploit the XYZ affair, Marshall won election by just over a hundred votes.[5] That the XYZ affair did not give any long-range political advantage to the Federalists can be seen by the election results of 1800. Instead, the XYZ affair produced a consensus that total separation from France was imperative, and war was unjustified.

The lasting importance of the XYZ affair was more significant than the eventual settlement of the dispute with France. The experience strengthened the attitude of many Americans that their country should have little to do with any European power. A contrary policy had been followed during the American Revolution, when members of the Continental Congress assumed that France would aid the United States for reasons of French self-interest. Despite their previous experience of warfare against France, the United States' first representatives abroad went straight to Paris to secure loans, ammunition, and skilled personnel for the American army. Later, after the Battle of Saratoga, the United States signed an entangling alliance with France that secured American independence.

France was seen as a counterweight to Great Britain's power. From the beginning of the Revolution until the XYZ affair, Americans sought recourse to another first-rate power to counteract the might of Great Britain. John Jay gained limited concessions from the British, partly because Great Britain did not want to be distracted by a war in the western world while facing the victorious French revolutionary armies in Europe. Because of their relations with France, Americans could make the British more cautious.

The political change wrought by the XYZ affair was to eliminate the idea of using France to counter Britain. France's transgressions meant that it could no longer be considered as a partner in any prospective conflict with Great Britain. Often accused by his opponents of being pro-French, Thomas Jefferson believed that the United States must maintain friendly ties with a power able and willing to go to war with Great Britain. But in his extensive campaign for the presidency in 1800, Jefferson chose not to discuss foreign affairs. He wanted peace, commerce, and union, and, of course, lower taxes. On assuming office, Jefferson announced in his inaugural address that he sought "Peace, Commerce, and honest friendship with all nations, entangling alliances with none."[6] Halfheartedly, Jefferson tried to reintroduce the French into the American theater by encouraging France to retake Haiti, even though this would mean reinstituting slavery and reversing Adams's policy of encouraging Haitian autonomy. When the French Haitian adventure failed and France began to seek to take control of Louisiana from Spain, Jefferson proclaimed that the United States must marry itself to the British fleet.

After 1805, when Great Britain reversed its policy toward neutrals, Jefferson did not call upon France or seriously contemplate working with that nation. The abortive Monroe-Pinckney Treaty of 1807 with Great Britain, and the ill-fated embargo as well, demonstrated that France no longer figured as a serious consideration in American strategy. Despite numerous charges by the Federalists, neither Madison nor Monroe as his secretary of state ever sought to coordinate American policy with France even through the War of 1812.[7]

The XYZ affair had other implications as well—effects that reveal the continuing tension of the 1790s throughout Europe and the United States. The publication of the envoys' dispatches was widely interpreted as a Federalist tactic to discredit the Republicans. The evidence for this contention is overwhelming, but another aspect of the publication of the dispatches is overlooked. Because of the French Revolution's widespread appeal, as it swept aside old forms of government, society, and diplomacy, governments had to assure a sizable number of their citizens that actual or threatened war with France reflected national interest rather than an ideological distrust of republicanism and revolution.

A study of the British negotiations with France at the same time offers parallels to much of United States policy from 1797 to 1799. Lord Malmesbury had been appointed to negotiate with the Directory in 1796, in part because of his known Whig views in opposition to a number of members of William Pitt's cabinet. The French broke off the negotiations, stating that the British did not truly desire peace. The following year Lord Malmesbury returned to

Lille to reopen the negotiations. These talks also failed because of disputes on the division and return of European colonial possessions in the middle of October 1797. The Pitt ministry then published extensive sections of the correspondence to try to convince the British public that the French were in fact demanding a diplomatic settlement more in the style of Louis XIV than that of a missionary revolutionary republic. Yet even after the second set of talks collapsed, Thomas Melville and Pierre Bellamy returned to London to see if the British were willing to open talks again. The British were still willing to explore the issues and deposited some of the demanded bribe money with a British banker in Paris. [8] At all times Pitt tried to assure his opponents that he was not pursuing a war to return the monarchy to France and destroy the French republic.

The Federalists' decision to publish the complete correspondence of the first mission to France was, in part, a response to Republican suspicions that the Adams administration wanted unduly harsh terms from France. The published dispatches had the advantage of being explicit in describing French demands that were both imperial and venal. Yet Adams made the decision in 1799 to renew the plans for peace, once again relying on his calculation of American interests, not on his own or his Federalist opponents' distaste for revolutionary republicanism. The second mission, which was successful, saw very little material published on the course of the negotiations.

Adams later stressed his own courage in averting war at the cost of his own political future. He chose to overlook those parts of his French policy, namely, the greatly increased defense spending, particularly on the army, and the notorious Alien and Sedition Acts, that contributed to his narrow defeat by Jefferson. The Republicans emphasized domestic issues in the 1800 election, attacking the glaring misuse of power under the Federalists. Certainly it was not the second mission to France that caused Adams's defeat. His downfall came from the passage and implementation of the program of defense in the summer of 1798, when the XYZ affair had given him temporary popularity.

The XYZ affair has often been interpreted in the context of honest Americans versus corrupt Frenchmen. Unfortunately, this emphasis ignores all substantive issues between France and the

United States. Rather than a consideration of the envoys' or the president's integrity and probity, we need to examine the issues and gains by the United States from their resolution. American commitments under the Jay Treaty continued, and no further commitments to France were made. Neutrality was preserved, and thus American merchants could continue to exploit the lucrative war market in Europe. By 1801 the only entangling alliance with a European power made in the United States' first 150 years had been abandoned.

The XYZ affair marked the beginning of a period in which Americans made concerted efforts to separate their own experiment from European practices. After the initial bribe request from the French, John Marshall had written that France "is not and never will be a republick is a truth which I scarcely dare whisper even to myself."[9] Marshall then expressed the feeling that Americans ever since the Revolution have wanted to believe about the role of the United States in international affairs: "It is in America and America only that human liberty has found an asylum. Let our foreign factions banish her from the United States and this earth affords her no longer a place of refuge."

Notes

1. The abundant literature on the question can be followed in Alexander DeConde, *The Quasi-War* (New York, 1966), Stephen G. Kurtz, *The Presidency of John Adams* (Philadelphia, 1957); James M. Smith, *Freedom's Fetters* (Ithaca, 1966); Marshall Smelser, "The Federalist Period as an Age of Passion," *American Quarterly* 10 (1958): 391-419.

2. Dauer, *The Adams Federalists*, 2d ed. (Baltimore, Md., 1968), pp. xxi-xxiii, summarized the argument very well.

3. Bradford Perkins, *The First Rapprochement* (Berkeley and Los Angeles, 1967), pp. 92-105.

4. Joel W. Keuhl, "Quest for Identity: The XYZ Affair and American Nationalism," Ph.D. diss., University of Wisconsin, 1968; see also Myron F. Wehtje, "The Congressional Elections in 1799 in Virginia," *West Virginia History* 29 (1968): 252, 257.

5. The best account of this election is Nancy M. Merz, "The XYZ Affair and the Congressional Election of 1799 in Richmond, Virginia," (M.A. thesis, College of William and Mary, 1973).

6. For his campaign statement, see Thomas Jefferson to Elbridge Gerry, 26 January 1799; quote from Inaugural Address, 4 March 1801, Thomas Jefferson Papers, Library of Congress, Washington, D.C.

7. Bradford Perkins, *Prologue to War, 1805-1812: England and the United States* (Berkeley and Los Angeles, 1961).

8. Third Earl of Malmesbury, *Diaries and Correspondence of James Harris, First Earl of Malmesbury*, 4 vols. (London, 1845), 3: 250-575; James Harris, First Earl of Malmesbury, *Correspondence officielle et complète de Lord Malmesbury, déposée sur le bureau des deux chambres du Parlement d'Angleterre, le 3 novembre, 1797* (Paris, 1797); Charles Ballot, *Les Négociations de Lille* (Paris, 1910), pp. 143, 237, 311.

9. John Marshall to Charles Lee, 12-[27] October 1797, "Diplomatic Despatches, France," 6, Record Group 59, National Archives, Washington, D.C.

Appendix

Americans in Paris, 1797-1798

Name	Occupation	Residence	Identification*
Solomon Abraham	Captain	Boston	P
Thomas Adams	Traveler	Boston	P
Otis Ammidon	Merchant		MP
James Anderson	Merchant	Charlestown, Md.	MP
John Andrews	Merchant	Boston	FG, MP, P, S
Samuel Andrews	Merchant	Boston	FG, MP, P, S
Nathaniel Appleton	Merchant-Consul**	Boston	
Thomas Appleton	Merchant	Boston	P
George W. Apthorp	Merchant	Boston	P
William R. Apthorp	Merchant	Boston	P
Charles W. Apthorp	Merchant	Boston	P
Richard Arden	Merchant		P
John Avery	Merchant	Boston	P
William Bache	Privateer	Philadelphia	
Berial Baker			
Joel Barlow	Land Merchant	Hartford	FG
Francis Barker	Merchant	North Carolina	P
Isaac Barnet	Merchant-Consul	New Jersey	

*Identification:
    FG – French Government Contract
    MP – Monroe Petition
    P – Passport
    S – Spoliation Claims

**Consuls are those appointed as United States Consuls between 1789-1801.

Name	Occupation	Residence	Identification*
Joshua Barney	Captain	Baltimore	
Samuel Barrett	Merchant-Consul	Boston	P, S
Jean F. Bernard	Merchant		P
John W. Billopp	Merchant		
Samuel Blackden	Land Merchant	Connecticut	
Eizale Blarrey	Merchant		P
Stephen Blyth	Merchant	Salem	MP
John Brockenbourgh	Land Merchant	Williamsburg	
Edward Bromfield	Merchant	Newburyport	
Samuel Broome	Merchant	Hartford	MP
Samuel Broome, Jr.	Merchant	Hartford	MP, P
John Brown	Diplomat	Richmond	
William Brown	Merchant	Norwich	
John Bryant	Merchant	Boston	MP
John Buffington	Merchant-Captain	Salem	MP, P
Thomas Bulkeley	Merchant	Boston	S
Thomas Bulkeley, Jr.	Merchant-Consul	Boston	S
Samuel Burley	Captain	Boston	
Walter Burling	Merchant	Boston	MP, P
John Calhoun	Merchant	Baltimore	
Benjamin Callander	Merchant	Boston	MP
David Cargill	Captain		P
Oliver Champlain	Captain		MP
Francis Childs	Consul	New York	P
Edward Church	Merchant-Consul	Boston	P
Edward Church, Jr.	Merchant	Boston	P
Sally Clenachem		Philadelphia	P
Stephen Clough	Captain	Wicassett	P
George Codeweisse	Merchant	New York	P
Richard Codman	Merchant	Boston	
Edmund Coffin	Merchant-Consul	Nantucket	S
Michael Connolly	Merchant	New York	P
William Constable	Merchant-Land	New York	
Peter Constantin	Merchant		P
Richard Cooke			P
Z. Coopman	Merchant	Baltimore	FG, MP, P
Samuel Cooper, Jr.	Captain	Philadelphia	
William Cullen	Merchant		P
Jacob Custis	Merchant	Petersburg	P
Nathaniel Cutting	Merchant-Consul	Boston	P

Name	Occupation	Residence	Identification*
William Cutting	Merchant	Boston	P
John Dabney	Merchant	Boston	P
Thomas Danforth	Merchant	Boston	MP
Louis d'Autremont	Land Merchant	Asylum	P
Paul d'Autremont	Land Merchant	Asylum	P
John Davidson	Captain	Annapolis	P
Samuel Dexter	Captain	Gloucester	
J. B. C. Dubuc			P
Pierpont Edwards	Land Merchant	Hartford	P
Calvin Elliott	Merchant		P
Hugh Elliott	Merchant		P
William Erand	Merchant		P
John Eustache	Soldier	New York	MP, P
George W. Erving	Merchant-Consul	Philadelphia	
John Fabre	Merchant		MP
Noel Faming	Merchant		MP
James Fenwick	Merchant-Consul	Georgetown	FG, P
John Fleming	Captain	Baltimore	MP, P
John Forbes	Merchant	Boston	MP
R. Bennett Forbes	Merchant	Boston	MP
Andrew Foster	Captain	New York	P
Bossenger Foster, Jr.	Diplomat-Land Merchant	Boston	
William T. Franklin	Land Merchant	Philadelphia	
Alexander Fraser	Captain	Boston	P
Stephen French	Merchant		MP
Henry Fulford	Merchant		MP
Robert Fulton	Artist	Philadelphia	FG
Samuel Fulton	Soldier	Kentucky	MP
John Gamble	Traveler	Richmond	
David Gelston	Merchant	New York	MP
Elbridge Gerry	Diplomat	Cambridge	
George Gibbs, Jr.	Merchant	Newport	MP
Joshua Gilpin	Merchant	Philadelphia	S
Thomas W. Griffith	Merchant-Consul	Baltimore	MP
John Griste	Merchant		MP
James Grubb	Merchant	Philadelphia	P, S
Robert Halen	Merchant		P
Miss Hall		Philadelphia	
Hartley	Merchant	New York	

Name	Occupation	Residence	Identification*
Solomon Haskill	Merchant	Newburyport	P, S
James Hemphill	Merchant	Philadelphia	P, S
John G. Heslop	Merchant		MP
Benjamin Hichborn	Land Merchant	Boston	FG
George Higginson	Student	Boston	
John Higginson	Merchant	Boston	FG, MP
Joshua Hill	Captain	Maryland	P
Benjamin Hiller			P
Joseph Hinkley	Merchant	Boston	P
Frances Hollingsworth	Merchant	Baltimore	MP
Robert Holn			P
John Homes	Merchant-Consul	Baltimore	MP
Giles Hommideau	Land Merchant	New York	
James Hooe	Merchant	Alexandria	
Samuel M. Hopkins	Land Merchant	Hartford	
William Hopkins	Merchant	Boston	
Charles P. Horry	Student	Charleston	
John Houghton	Merchant	Philadelphia	MP, P
G. Howell	Merchant	Pennsylvania	MP
Clement Humphries	Diplomat	Philadelphia	
Joseph Ingraham	Captain-Consul	Boston	
George Izard	Student	Charleston	
Ralph Izard, Jr.	Student	Charleston	
Edward James			P
Isaac Jameson	Soldier	Kentucky	MP, P
Benjamin Jarvis	Merchant		FG
John Jeffrey	Captain	Norfolk	P
Benjamin Johnson			P
Henry Johnson	Captain	Boston	MP, P
William Johnson	Merchant		P
John Kidder	Merchant	Boston	
Cyrus King	Traveler	New York	
Thomas Lang	Merchant		MP
Mark Leavenworth	Land Merchant	Hartford	MP
William Lee	Merchant	Salem	MP
James LeRay	Land Merchant	New York	P
J. R. Livingston	Merchant	New York	FG
Robert J. Livingston	Merchant	New York	MP, P
J. Lovette	Captain	New York	
Isaac Low	Merchant	New York	

Name	Occupation	Residence	Identification*
William Lowry	Merchant	Baltimore	MP
Daniel Ludlow	Merchant	New York	S
George Lyle		New Jersey	P
Robert Lyle	Merchant	New Jersey	MP, P
Samuel Lyle		New Jersey	P
Theodore Lyman, Jr.	Merchant	Boston	P, S
William Lynch	Merchant		P
Elizabeth Moore Barbé-Marbois		Philadelphia	
James Marshall	Land Merchant	Philadelphia	
John Marshall	Diplomat	Richmond	
Louis Marshall	Land Merchant	Kentucky	MP, P
John Martin	Merchant		
Joseph Maule	Merchant	New York	
Ebenezer May	Merchant		MP, P
Richard Meade	Merchant	Philadelphia	FG
Thomas Melville, Jr.	Banker	Boston	MP
David Meredith	Merchant	Philadelphia	P
Henry Middleton	Student	Charleston	MP
John Mitchell	Captain	New York	MP
William Morris	Land Merchant	Philadelphia	
James Mountflorence	Land Merchant	Knoxville	FG, MP
John Muir	Merchant	Annapolis	MP, S
George Murray	Merchant	New York	FG, MP
James V. Murray	Merchant	New York	FG
John B. Murray	Merchant	New York	FG, MP
Jonathan Nesbitt	Merchant	Philadelphia	FG, MP
Samuel Norwood	Merchant		MP
Michael O'Mealy	Merchant	Baltimore	FG
Thomas Paine	Writer	Philadelphia	MP
Daniel Parker	Merchant	Boston	MP
John Parker	Merchant	Boston	MP
J. Peters	Merchant		
Oliver Phelps, Jr.	Land Merchant	New York	MP
Hezekiah Pierpont	Merchant	New York	S
Charles C. Pinckney	Diplomat	Charleston	
Joseph Pitcairn	Merchant-Consul	New York	
Henry Platt	Merchant	Portland	P
Zaphanah Platt	Merchant	New York	
Henry Preble	Merchant	Portland	

Name	Occupation	Residence	Identification*
Henry Prevost		New York	
James Prince	Merchant	Newburyport	P, S
John Purviance	Merchant	Baltimore	
Jesse Putnam	Merchant	Boston	MP
Charles Pye			
Thomas Ramsden	Merchant	Salem	MP
Charles Rogers	Merchant	Newburyport	P, S
James Rogers	Merchant	Newburyport	P, S
Joseph Rogers	Merchant-Captain	Newburyport	S
William Rogers	Merchant	Newburyport	P, S
Francis Rotch	Merchant	Nantucket	MP
Joseph Russell	Merchant	Boston	MP, P
Thomas Russell	Merchant	Boston	
Robert Rutgert		New York	
Henry Rutledge, Jr.	Diplomat	Charleston	
States Rutledge	Student	Charleston	
Henry Sadler, Jr.	Merchant	New York	
Joseph Sands	Merchant	New York	MP
Abraham Sasportas	Merchant	Charleston	
William Short	Diplomat	Williamsburg	
Richard Skinner	Merchant	Boston	
Fulwar Skipwith	Merchant-Consul	Williamsburg	MP, S
Gideon Snow	Captain	Boston	
Deward Starbuck	Merchant	Nantucket	
Daniel Strobel	Merchant	Boston	MP
James Swan	Merchant	Boston	MP
William Talcott	Merchant	Hartford	S
Frances Taney	Merchant	Baltimore	P
Samuel Tarbell			P
William Tate	Soldier	Charleston	
William Tazewell	Diplomat	Williamsburg	
James Thayer	Merchant	Charleston	
Abraham Thomas	Captain	New York	P
D. Thompson			MP, P
Elizabeth Thompson			P
Hugh Thompson	Merchant	Baltimore	P
Frederick Thorwill			P
David Tilden	Merchant	Boston	P, S
David Tilden, Jr.	Merchant	Boston	S
James Tisdale	Merchant	Boston	P

Name	Occupation	Residence	Identification*
Hare B. Trist	Merchant	Philadelphia	
Nicholas Trist	Merchant	Philadelphia	
John Trumbull	Artist	Hartford	
William Tudor	Merchant	Boston	MP, P
Benjamin Tupper	Merchant	Boston	MP
John Vaché	Merchant		MP, P
John Vanderlyn	Student	Kingston	MP
William Vans	Merchant-Consul	Salem	MP
William Vernon, Jr.	Merchant	Newport	MP
J. Vouchez	Merchant		MP
James Wadsworth	Land Merchant	Geneseo	
A. Waldryhm	Soldier	Kentucky	MP
Ephriam Wales			MP
Benjamin Walker	Land Merchant	New York	MP
Z. Walker	Merchant	New York	MP
James Watson	Land Merchant	New York	
John Wheeler			MP
Peter Whiteside	Merchant	Philadelphia	
Joseph Whittemore	Merchant	New York	MP
Thomas Willard	Merchant		MP
Samuel Williams	Merchant-Banker	Boston	
Henry Worthington	Merchant		MP

Bibliography

Manuscripts

American Antiquarian Society, Worcester, Massachusetts:
    Andrew Craigie Papers
Archives du Ministère des Affaires Étrangères, Paris
    Correspondance Politique: Angleterre, vols. 590-592
                      États-Unis, vols. 43-51
                      Hamburg, vols. 108-13
                      Hollande, vols. 595-98
    Correspondance Politique. États-Unis, Supplement, vols. 2, 5, 19, 21-25, 31, 36, 37
    Correspondance Politique États-Unis, Mémoires et Documents. vols. 2, 5, 6, 9, 10
    Correspondance Politique: États-Unis: Consular New York, vol. 3, 1793-1805
    DeSages, vol. 36
Archives Nationales, Paris
    AF^{II} vol. 53
    AF*^{II} vols. 177, 234
    AF^{III} vols. 56, 64, 625
    AF*^{III} vols. 146, 153, 156, 175-79, 246
    F^{7} vols. 80, 642, 2205, 2207, 4269, 4591, 4594, 4598, 4652, 4720, 4722, 4733, 4744, 4751, 4774, 4775, 4779, 6141, 6152, 6167, 6168, 6214, 6374, 6608
Chicago Historical Society, Chicago, Illinois:
    Ward Family Papers
Cincinnati Historical Society, Cincinnati, Ohio:
    Joseph Pitcairn Papers
College of William and Mary, Williamsburg, Virginia:
    John Marshall Papers
    Tucker-Coleman Papers

Connecticut Historical Society, Hartford, Connecticut:
    Oliver Wolcott Papers
Duke University, Durham, North Carolina:
    John Clopton Papers
Eleutherian Mills Historical Library, Wilmington, Delaware:
    D'Autremont Family Papers
    DuPont Family Papers
Free Library of Philadelphia, Philadelphia, Pennsylvania:
    Autograph Letters
Gemeentearchief, Amsterdam:
    Brants Archives
    Holland Land Company Papers
Harvard University, Cambridge, Massachusetts:
    Autograph Letters
    Joel Barlow Papers
Henry E. Huntington Library, San Marino, California:
    Elbridge Gerry Papers
    Rufus King Papers
Historical Society of Pennsylvania, Philadelphia, Pennsylvania:
    Conarroe Papers
    Dreer Collection
    Gilpin Papers
    John W. Godfrey Diary
    Gratz Collection
    Clement Humphries Papers
    Scioto Land Company Manuscripts
Library of Congress, Washington, D.C.:
    Sylvanus Bourne Papers
    Causten-Pickett Papers
    Elbridge Gerry Papers
    Thomas Jefferson Papers
    Rufus King Papers
    Lee-Palfrey Papers
    James Madison Papers
    John Marshall Papers
    James Monroe Papers
    Gouverneur Morris Papers
    Robert Morris Papers
    William Vans Murray Papers
    Pinckney Family Papers
    William Short Papers
    William L. Smith Papers

John Trumbull Papers
George Washington Papers
Louisiana State University, Baton Rouge, Louisiana:
    Fulwar Skipwith Papers
Massachusetts Historical Society, Boston, Massachusetts:
    Adams Family Papers
    Nathaniel Cutting Papers
    Gerry Papers
    Thomas Jefferson Papers
    Knight-Gerry Papers
    Henry Knox Papers
    Thomas H. Perkins Papers
    Timothy Pickering Papers
    Smith Carter Papers
National Archives, Washington, D.C.:
    Record Group 46: Records of the United States; Records of Executive Proceedings, Executive Nominations, and Accompanying Papers.
    Record Group 53: Records of Bureau of Accounts.
    Record Group 59: General Records of the Department of State:
        Despatches from United States Consuls in Leghorn, 1793-1806
        Despatches from United States Consuls in Paris: 1790-1805
        Despatches from United States Consuls in Bordeaux, 1789-1803
        Diplomatic and Consular Instructions of the Department of State, 1791-1801
        Domestic Letterbooks
        Diplomatic Despatches: France, Great Britain, Netherlands, and Spain.
        Miscellaneous Letters, M-179.
    Record Group 76: American Commission, Paris, 1803.
    Record Group 84: Correspondence, American Embassy, Paris.
New-York Historical Society, New York, New York:
    Albert Gallatin Papers
    Rufus King Papers
    Robert R Livingston Papers
    John Trumbull Papers
New York Public Library, New York, New York:
    Constable Pierpont Papers
    Emmet Collection
New York State Library, Albany, New York:
    Phelps-Gorham Papers
North Carolina State Archives, Raleigh, North Carolina:
    William Davie Papers

Pennsylvania Historical and Museum Commission, Harrisburg,
Pennsylvania:
  Joshua and Thomas Gilpin Papers
Pierpont Morgan Library, New York, New York:
  Elbridge Gerry Papers
  William Vans Murray Papers
Private Archives, Paris
Senate and House Museum, Kingston, New York:
  John Vanderlyn Papers
South Carolina Historical Society, Charleston, South Carolina:
  Pinckney Papers
University of Rochester, Rochester, New York:
  James Wadsworth Papers
University of South Carolina, Columbia, South Carolina:
  Manigault Family Papers
Yale University, New Haven, Connecticut:
  Joel Barlow Papers
  Franklin Collection: Legation Book, 1797-1798
  Roger Griswold Papers
  John Trumbull Papers

Primary Printed Sources

Adams, Charles F., ed. *The Works of John Adams,* 10 vols. Boston: Little, Brown & Company, 1850-1856.
Allis, Frederick, Jr., ed. *William Bingham's Maine Lands,* 2 vols. Boston: Colonial Society of Massachusetts, 1954.
Armentrout, Virginia and James, eds. *The Diary of Harriet Manigault.* Philadelphia: The Colonial Dames of America, 1976.
Bailleu, Paul, ed., *Preussen und Frankreich von 1795 bis 1807: Diplomatische Correspondenzen,* 2 vols. Leipzig: Neudruck der Ausgabe, 1881-1887.
Balayé Simon, ed. *Lettres à Ribbing.* Paris: Gallimard, 1960.
Barck, Dorothy C., ed. *Diary of William Dunlap,* 4 vols. New York: New-York Historical Society, 1929.
Boyd, Julian et al., eds. *The Papers of Thomas Jefferson,* 19 vols to date. Princeton, N.J.: Princeton University Press, 1950-.
Broglie, Duke de, ed., "Lettres de M. Talleyrand à Madame de Staël." *Revue d'Histoire Diplomatique* 6 (1890): 209-21.
Browning, Oscar, ed. *The Despatches of Earl Grower.* Cambridge: Cambridge University Press, 1885.

Bury, J. B. T. and Barry, J. C., eds. *An Englishman in Paris: The Journal of Bertie Greatheed.* London: Bles, 1953.

Cazenove, A. de, ed. *Journal de Madame de Cazenove d'Arlens.* Paris: Alphonse Picard et Fils, 1903.

Cramer, Lucien, ed. *Une famille genevoise, Les Cramers.* Geneva: E. Droz, 1952.

Cronin, James E., ed. *The Diary of Elihu Hubbard Smith.* Philadelphia: American Philosophical Society, 1978.

Cunningham, Noble E., ed. *Circular Letters of Congressmen to their Constituents: 1789-1829*, 3 vols. Chapel Hill, N.C.: University of North Carolina Press, 1978.

Davenport, Beatrix C., ed. *A Diary of the French Revolution*, 2 vols. Boston: Houghton Mifflin & Company, 1939.

Debates and Proceedings in the Congress of the United States, 1789-1825. Washington: Gales & Seaton, 1834-1856.

Delacroix, Charles, *Des Moyens de régénrer la France.* Paris: F. Buisson, Imprimeur Libraire, 1797.

Diary of William Bentley, 4 vols. Salem, Mass.: Essex Institute, 1905-1914.

DuPont, Victor. *Journey to France and Spain.* Edited by Charles W. David. Ithaca, N.Y. Cornell University Press, 1961.

Fauchet, Joseph. "Mémoire sur les États-Unis d'Amérique." Edited by Carl Lokke. American Historical Association, *Annual Report*, 1935. Washington, D.C., 1938, 1.

Foner, Philip, ed. *The Writings of Thomas Paine*, 2 vols. New York: Citadel Press, 1969.

French Spoliations Prior to the Year 1800. House of Representatives Document 182, 24th Congress, 2nd Session. Washington, D.C., 1838.

French Spoliations to 1800. House Report 343, 26th Congress, 1st Session. Washington, D.C., 1840.

French Spoliations to 1800. House Report 116, 27th Congress, 2nd Session. Washington, 1841.

Fauchet, Joseph. *A Sketch of the Present State of our Political Relations with the United States of North America.* Philadelphia: Benjamin Franklin Bache, 1797.

Grandmaison, Geoffroy de, ed. *Correspondence du Comte de La Forest,* 8 vols. Paris: Alphonse Picard et Fils, 1905-1914.

Harris, James, First Earl of Malmesbury. *Correspondence officielle et complète de Lord Malmesbury, deposée sur le bureau des deux chambres de Parlement d'Angleterre, le 3 Novembre, 1797.* Paris: L'Imprimerie des Amis Reunis, 1797.

Hemlow, Joyce, ed. *The Journals and Letters of Fanney Burney: Madame d'Arblay*, 6 vols. to date. Oxford: Oxford University Press, 1972-.

Huth, Hans and Wilma Pugh, eds. *Talleyrand in America as a Financial Promoter.* Washington, D.C.: American Historical Society, 1942.

Keith, Alice B. and Masterson, William, eds. *The John Gray Blount Papers,* 3 vols. Raleigh, N.C.: North Carolina State Archives, 1952-1965.

Keith, Alice B., ed. "Letters from Major James Cole Mountflorence to Members of the Blount Family." *North Carolina Historical Review* 14 (1937): 251-87.

Knight, Russell W., ed. *Elbridge Gerry's Letterbook: Paris, 1797-1798.* Salem, Mass.: Essex Institute, 1966.

Lettres au Docteur Priestly en Amerique. London: N.P., 1798.

McCombs, Charles R., ed. *Letterbook of Mary Stead Pinckney: November 14, 1796 to August 29, 1797.* New York: Gilmor Club, 1946.

McIntosh, M. E. and Weber, B. C., eds. *Une Correspondance Familiale au Temps des Troubles de Saint-Domingue.* Paris: Sociéte de l'Histoire des Colonies Français et Librarie Larose, 1959.

Malmesbury, Lord, 3rd Earl of, ed. *Diaries and Correspondence of James Harris, First Earl of Malmesbury,* 4 vols. London: R. Bentley, 1845.

Mathiez, Albert, ed. "Letters de Volney à Revellière-Lépeaux," *Annales Révolutionnaires* 3 (1910): 161-94.

Marchand, Jean, ed. *Journal de Voyage en Amérique et d'un Sojour à Philadelphie.* Baltimore & Paris: Johns Hopkins University Press & R. Craveuil, 1940.

Marshall, James F., ed. and trans. *Correspondence of Madame de Staël and Pierre Samuel DuPont de Nemours.* Madison, Wisc.: University of Wisconsin Press, 1968.

Marshall, P. J., McDowell, R. B., and Woods, John, eds. *The Correspondence of Edmund Burke,* vols 7-9. Cambridge: Cambridge University Press, 1968-1970.

Message of the President of the United States submitted to both Houses of Congress, April 3, 1798. Philadelphia: Printed by order of the United States Senate, 1798.

Monroe, James. *A View of the Conduct of the Executive.* Philadelphia: Benjamin Franklin Bache, 1797.

Niemcewicz, Julian V. *Under Their Vine and Fig Tree.* Edited and translated by Metchie J. C. Budka. Elizabeth, N.J.: Grassman Publishing Co., 1965.

Official and Private Correspondence of Major-General J. S. Eustace, 3 vols. Paris: Privately Printed, 1796.

Otto, Louis, *Considérations sur la Conduite de Gouvernement Américain envers la France depuis la Commencement de la Révolution jusqu'en 1797.* Edited by Gilbert Chinard. Princeton, N.J.: Princeton University Press, 1945.

Pallain, G., ed. "Les États-Unis en Angleterre en 1795." *Revue d'Histoire Diplomatique* 3 (1889): 64-77.

Pickering, Timothy. *A Review of the Correspondence between the Honorable John Adams and the late William Cunningham,* 2 ed. Salem, Mass.: Privately Printed, 1824.

Saint-Méry, Moreau de. *Voyage aux États-Unis d'Amérique, 1793-1798.* Edited by Stewart L. Mims. New Haven, Conn.: Yale University Press, 1913.

Sawvel, Franklin B., ed. *The Complete Anas of Thomas Jefferson.* New York: DeCapo Press, 1970.

Stinchcombe, William and Charles T. Cullen, eds. *The Papers of John Marshall,* 3 vols. Chapel Hill, N.C.: University of North Carolina Press, 1979.

Syrett, Harold, et al., eds. *The Papers of Alexander Hamilton,* 26 vols. New York: Columbia University Press, 1961-1979.

Talleyrand, Charles M. "Commercial Relations of the United States with England" and "An Essay upon the Advantages to be Derived from New Colonies." Boston: Thomas B. Wait, 1809.

Tone, William T. F., ed. *The Memoirs of Theobald Wolfe Tone.* London: H. Colburn, 1837.

Turner, Frederick J., ed. *Correspondence of the French Ministers.* Washington, D.C.: American Historical Association, 1904.

Watson, Wimslow, ed. *Memoirs of Elkanah Watson.* New York: Dana & Company, 1857.

Newspapers

Alexandria Times

[Boston] *Columbian Centinel*

[Boston] *Independent Chronicle*

Columbian Mirror and Alexandria Gazette

[Hartford] *Connecticut Courant*

[Paris] *Le Moniteur Universel*

[Philadelphia] *Aurora*

[Philadelphia] *Gazette & Universal Daily Advertiser*

[Philadelphia] *Gazette of the United States*
[Philadelphia] *Claypoole's American Daily Advertiser*
[Philadelphia] *Porcupine's Gazette*
[Philadelphia] *Pennsylvania Gazette*
[Philadelphia] *Courrier Français*
[Richmond] *Virginia Argus*
[Richmond] *Virginia Gazette and General Advertiser*
Salem Gazette

Secondary Sources

Alberts, Robert C. *The Golden Voyage: The Life and Times of William Bingham: 1752-1804.* Boston: Houghton Mifflin & Company, 1969.

Alger, John. *Englishmen in the French Revolution* London: S. Low, Movston, Searle & Rivington, 1889.

————. *Paris, 1789-1794.* London: G. Allen, 1902.

Ammon, Harry. *James Monroe.* New York: McGraw Hill, 1971.

Austin, James T. *Life of Elbridge Gerry,* 2 vols. New York: DeCapo Press, 1970.

Baldridge, Edwin R. "Talleyrand's Visit to Pennsylvania, 1794-1796." *Pennsylvania History* 36 (1969): 145-60.

Ballot, Charles. *Les Négociations de Lille.* Paris: Édouard Cornély et Cie., 1910.

Beckham, Stephen D. "Colonel George Gibbs." In *Benjamin Silliman and His Circle,* edited by Leonard C. Wilson. New York: Science History Publications, 1979.

Beveridge, Albert. *The Life of John Marshall,* 4 vols. Boston: Houghton Mifflin Company, 1916-1919.

Billias, George. *Elbridge Gerry.* New York: McGraw-Hill, 1976.

Bizardel, Yvon. *American Painters in Paris.* Translated by Richard Howard, New York: MacMillan & Company, 1960.

————. "French Estates, American Landlords." Translated by Florence Yorke. *Apollo* 101(1975): 108-15.

————*Les Américains à Paris pendant la Révolution.* Paris: Calmann-Levy, 1972.

Bond, Beverly W., Jr. *The Monroe Mission to France.* Baltimore, Md.: Johns Hopkins University Press, 1907.

Bonnel, Ulane A. *La France et États-Unis et la guerre de course: 1799-1815.* Paris: Nouvelles Editions latine, 1961.

Bosher, J. F. *French Finances: 1770-1795.* Cambridge, England: Cambridge University Press, 1970.

Bouchary, J. "Les compagnies financières à Paris à la fin du XVIIIe Siécle." *Annales Historiques de la Révolution Française* 17 (1940): 129-50.

Bowman, Albert H. *The Struggle for Neutrality.* Knoxville, Tenn.: University of Tennessee Press, 1974.

Boyce, Myrna. "The Diplomatic Career of William Short." *Journal of Modern History* 15(1943): 97-119.

Boyer, Ferdinand. "Une Conquête Artistique de la Convention: Les Tableaux du Stathouder: 1795." *Bulletin de la Société de L'Histoire de l'Art Française* (1970): 149-57.

————. "Les Responsabilités de Napoléon dans le transfert à Paris des oeuvres d'art de l'*étranger.*" *Revue d'Histoire Moderne et Contemporaine* 11(1964): 241-62.

Brace, Richard M. "Talleyrand in New England: Reality and Legend." *New England Quarterly* 16 (1943): 397-406.

Brown, Esther, *The French Revolution and the American Man of Letters.* Columbia, Missouri: University of Missouri Studies, 1951.

Bruchey, Stuart W., *Robert Oliver, Merchant of Baltimore: 1783-1819.* Baltimore, Md.: Johns Hopkins University Press, 1956.

Buel, Richard, Jr. *Securing the Revolution: Ideology in American Politics: 1789-1815.* Ithaca, N.Y.: Cornell University Press, 1972.

Buist, Martin. *At Spes Non Fracta: Hope & Company, 1770-1815.* The Netherlands: Martinus Nijhoff, 1974.

Burnet, Edouard L. *Le Premier Tribunal Révolutionnaire Genvois* Genève: La Societè d'Histoire et d'Archéologie de Genève, 1925.

Butel, Paul. *Les négociants bordelais, l'Europe et les Iles au XVIIIe Siècle* Paris: Aubier-Montaigne, 1974.

Charles, Joseph. *The Origins of the American Party System.* New York: Harper & Row, 1956.

Childs, Francis S. "A Secret Agent's Advice on America, 1797." In *Nationalism and Internationalism: Essays Inscribed to Carlton J. H. Hayes,* edited by Edward M. Earle. New York: Columbia University Press, 1950.

————. *French Refugee Life in the United States: 1790-1800.* Baltimore, Md.: Johns Hopkins University Press, 1940.

————. "The Hauterive Journal." *New-York Historical Society Quarterly* 33 (1949): 69-86.

Clarfield, Gerald. *Timothy Pickering and American Diplomacy.* Columbia, Missouri: University of Missouri Press, 1969.

Cooke, Jacob E. *Tench Coxe and the Early Republic.* Chapel Hill, N.C.: University of North Carolina Press, 1978.

Dauer, Manning J. *The Adams Federalists*, 2d ed. Baltimore, Md.: Johns Hopkins University Press, 1968.

Debien, Gabriel. *Les Colons de Saint-Domingue et la Révolution.* Paris: Armand Colin, 1953.

———. *Études Antillaises.* Paris: Armand Colin, 1956.

DeConde, Alexander. *Entangling Alliance: Politics and Diplomacy under Washington.* Durham, N.C.: Duke University Press, 1958.

———. *The Quasi-War.* New York: Charles Scribner's Sons, 1966.

Desnoiresterres, Gustave. *Voltaire et la Société au XVIIIᵉ Siècle* 2d. ed., 8 vols. Paris: Didier et Cie, 1871-1876.

Dexter, Franklin B., ed. *Biographical Sketches of Graduates of Yale, 1778-1792.* New York: Henry Holt & Company, 1907.

Durden, Robert. "Joel Barlow in the French Revolution." *William and Mary Quarterly* 8 (1951): 327-54.

Earl, John L., III. "Talleyrand in Philadelphia." *Pennsylvania Magazine of History and Biography.* 91(1967): 282-98.

Echeverria, Durand, ed. and trans. "General Collot's Plan for Reconnaissance of the Ohio and Mississippi Valleys, 1796." *William and Mary Quarterly* 9 (1952): 512-20.

———. *Mirage in the West.* Princeton, N.J.: Princeton University Press, 1957.

Ernst, Robert. *Rufus King: American Federalist.* Chapel Hill, N.C.: University of North Carolina Press, 1957.

Fajn, Max. "Le Journal des hommes libres de tous les pays' et les relations diplomatiques entre la France et les États-Unis de 1792 à 1800. *Revue d'Histoire Diplomatique* 85 (1971): 116-26.

Fay, Bernard. *L'Espirit revolutionnaire en France et Les Etats-Unis à la fin du XVIIIᵉ Sièle.* Paris: E. Champion, 1925.

Flexner, James. *George Washington*, 4 vols. Boston: Little Brown & Company, 1965-1972.

Footner, Hulbert. *Sailor of Fortune: The Life and Adventures of Commodore Barney, U.S.N.* New York: Harper & Brothers, 1940.

Fulton, John F. and Elizabeth H. Thomson. *Benjamin Silliman: Pathfinder in American Science.* New York: Greenwood Press, 1968.

Galiffe, Jacques. *Notices Généalogiques sur les Familles Genevoises.* 3 vols. Genève: H. Georg, 1836.

Gibbs, George Jr. *The Administration of Washington and Adams* 2 vols. New York: W. Van Norden, 1856.

Godechot, Jacques. *The Counter-Revolution: Doctrine and Action: 1789-1804.* Translated by Salvatore Attanasio. New York: Howard Fertig, 1971.

Gottesman, Rita S., ed. *The Arts and Crafts in New York: 1800-1804.* New York: New-York Historical Society, 1965.

Greene, John C. and John G. Burke. *The Science of Minerals in the Age of Jefferson.* Philadelphia: American Philosophical Society, 1978.

Guyot, Raymond. *Le Directoire et la Paix de l'Europe.* Paris: Félix Alcan, 1911.

Henderson, Helen W. *The Pennsylvania Academy of Fine Arts.* Boston: L. C. Page & Co., 1911.

Hill, Peter P. "Prologue to the Quasi-War: Stresses in Franco-American Commercial Relations, 1793-1796." *Journal of Modern History* 49 (1977): Microfiche D 1039.

————. *William Vans Murray.* Syracuse, N.Y. Syracuse University Press, 1971.

Humphreys, Letitia A. "Diary of Clement Humphreys of Philadelphia." *Pennsylvania Magazine of History and Biography* 32 (1908) 34-53.

Jaffe, Irma. *John Trumbull.* Boston: New York Graphic Society, 1975.

James, James A. *The Life of George Rogers Clark.* Chicago: University of Chicago Press, 1929.

Johnson, Allen and Dumas Malone, eds., *Dictionary of American Biography* 21 vols. New York: Charles Scribner's Sons, 1931.

Kaplan, Lawrence S. "France and Madison's Decision for War, 1812." *Mississippi Valley Historical Review* 50(1964): 652-71.

————. *Jefferson and France.* New Haven, Conn.: Yale University Press, 1967.

————. "Toward Isolationism: The Rise and Fall of the Franco-American Alliance, 1775-1801." In *The American Revolution and "A Candid World,"* edited by Lawrence S. Kaplan. Kent, Ohio: Kent State University Press, 1977.

Kennett, Lee. "John Shey Eustace and the French Revolution." *American Society of Legion of Honor Magazine* 45(1974) 29-43.

Ketcham, Ralph. *James Madison.* New York: Macmillan & Company, 1971.

Kramer, Eugene. "John Adams, Elbridge Gerry and the Origins of the XYZ Affair." *Essex Institute Historical Collections* 94 (1958): 57-68.

Kurtz, Stephen G. "The French Mission of 1799-1800: Concluding Chapter in the Statecraft of John Adams." *Political Science Quarterly* 80 (1965): 543-57.

————. *The Presidency of John Adams: The Collapse of Federalism, 1795-1800*. Philadelphia: University of Pennsylvania Press, 1957.

Kyte, George W. "A Spy on the Western Waters: The Military Intelligence Mission of General Collot in 1796." *Mississippi Valley Historical Review* 34 (1947): 427-42.

————. "The Detention of General Collot: A Sidelight on Anglo-American Relations, 1798-1800." *William and Mary Quarterly* 6 (1949): 628-30.

LaCour-Gayet, Georges. *Talleyrand*, 4 vols. Paris: Payot, 1930-1933.

Latimer, Elizabeth A. *My Scrap-Book of the French Revolution* Chicago: A. C. McClung & Company, 1898.

LeClerc, Lucien. "La Trahison des Colons Aristocrates de Sainte-Domingue en 1793-1794." *Annales Historiques de la Révolution Française*, 11 (1934): 348-60.

LeFebvre, Georges. *The French Revolution*. Translated by John H. Stewart and James Friguglietti. New York: Columbia University Press, 1964.

————. *The Thermidorians and the Directory*. Translated by Robert Baldick. New York: Columbia University Press, 1964.

LeRoy, J. Rutgers. "Inscriptions on the Tombstones of Americans Buried in Père la Chaise Cemetery, Paris, France." *Pennsylvania Magazine of History and Biography* 43 (1919): 251-56.

Lindsay, Kenneth C. *The Works of John Vanderlyn*. Binghamton, N.Y.: State University Press of New York, 1970.

Lodge, Henry C., ed. *Life and Letters of George Cabot*. Boston: Little, Brown & Company, 1877.

Lokke, Carl L. "The Trumbull Episode: A prelude to the 'XYZ' Affair." *New England Quarterly* 7 (1934): 100-14.

————. "Pourquoi Talleyrand ne fut pas Envoyé à Constantinople." *Annales Historiques de la Révolution Française*. 10 (1933): 153-59.

————. "New Light on London Merchant Investment in St. Dominique." *Hispanic American Historical Review*. 22 (1942): 670-76.

Lüthy, Herbert. *La Banque Protestante en France*, 2 vols. Paris: S.E.V.P.E.N., 1961.

Lyman, Theodore. *The Diplomacy of the United States*, 2 vols. Boston: Wills & Lilly, 1826.

Lyon, E. Wilson. "The Directory and the United States." *American Historical Review* 43 (1938): 514-32.

————. *Louisiana in French Diplomacy: 1759-1804*. Norman, Okla.: University of Oklahoma Press, 1934.

Malo, Henri. *Le Beau Montrond*. Paris: Émile-Paul, 1926.

Mathiez, Albert. *"Talon et la Police de Bonaparte."* Annales Historiques de la Révolution Française 5 (1928): 1-21.

Malone, Dumas. *Jefferson and the Ordeal of Liberty.* Boston: Little, Brown & Company, 1962.

Mann, Mary Lee. *A Yankee Jeffersonian: Selections from the Diary and Letters of William Lee of Massachusetts.* Cambridge: Harvard University Press, 1958.

Masson, Frédéric. *Le Départment des Affaires Étrangères pendant la Révolution.* Paris: E. Plon & Cie., 1877.

McKee, Christopher. *Edward Preble, 1761-1807.* Annapolis, Md.: Naval Institute Press, 1972.

Michaud, L. G., ed. *Biographie Universelle* 2d ed., 85 vols. Paris: Michaud Frères, 1811-1862.

Missoffe, Michel, "Le Prince recoit." In *Talleyrand,* edited by Jacques de Lacretelle. Paris: Librarie Hachette, 1964.

Mooney, Chase C. *William H. Crawford.* Lexington, Ky.: University of Kentucky Press, 1974.

Morison, Samuel E. "DuPont, Talleyrand, and the French Spoliations." Massachusetts Historical Society *Proceedings 49* (1915-1916): 63-79.

Müntz, Eugene. "Les Annexions de Collections d'art ou de Bibliothèques." *Revue d'Histoire Diplomatique* 9 (1895): 375-93; 10 (1896): 481-508.

Murray, Elsie. "French Experiments in Pioneerings in Northern Pennsylvania." *Pennsylvania Magazine of History and Biography* 68 (1944): 175-88.

Narbonne, Bernard. *Le Diplomatie du Directorie et Bonaparte d'après les Inedits de Reubell.* Paris: La Nouvelle Édition, 1951.

Norton, Mary B. *The British Americans: The Loyalist Exiles in London, 1774-1789.* Boston: Little Brown & Company, 1972.

Nussbaum, Frederick L. *Commercial Policy in the French Revolution: A Study in the Career of G. J. A. Ducher.* Washington, D.C.: American Historical Association, 1925.

Ott, Thomas O., *The Haitian Revolution: 1789-1804.* Knoxville, Tenn.: University of Tennessee Press, 1973.

Pallain, Georges, ed., *Le Ministère de Talleyrand sous le Directorie.* Paris: E. Plon & Cie, 1891.

Palmer, Robert R. *The Age of the Democratic Revolution,* 2 vols. Princeton, N.J.: Princeton University Press, 1959, 1964.

Palmer, Robert R. "Herman Melville et la Révolution Française," *Annales Historiques de la Révolution Française* 26 (1954): 254-56.

Perkins, Bradford, *Prologue to War: England and the United States, 1805-1812*. Berkeley, Calif.: University of California, 1961.

———. *The First Rapprochement*. Berkeley and Los Angeles: University of California Press, 1967.

Perkins, Samuel G. "Insurrection in St. Domingo," Massachusetts Historical Society *Proceedings* 2(1886): 305-90.

Pitcher, Donald. "Colonel James Swan and his French Furniture." *Antiques 37* (1940): 69-72.

Porter, Kenneth W., ed. *The Jacksons and the Lees*, 2 vols. New York: Russell & Russell, 1969.

Réau, Louis. *L'Art Francais aux États-Unis*. Paris: H. Lourens, 1926.

Reinhard, Marcel. *Le Grand Carnot*, 2 vols. Paris: Hachette, 1950-1952.

———. "Les Négociations de Lille et la Crise du 18 Fructidor d'après la Correspondance inédite de Colchen." *Revue d'histoire Moderne et Contemporaine* 5(1958): 39-56.

Rice, Howard., Jr. *Thomas Jefferson's Paris*. Princeton, N.J.: Princeton University Press, 1976.

———. "Documents sur le commerce avec les neutres en l'an II et III." *Annales Historiques de la Révolution Française* 17 (1940): 166-183.

———. "James Swan: Agent of the French Republic." *New England Quarterly* 10 (1937): 464-86.

———. "A Pair of Sèvres Vases," [Boston] *Bulletin of the Museum of Fine Arts* 55 (1957): 31-37.

———. "Notes on the Swan Furniture." [Boston] *Bulletin of the Museum of Fine Arts* 38(1940):43-48.

Robison, Georgia. *Revelllière-Lépeaux, Citizen Director*. New York: Columbia University Press, 1938.

Rogers, George., Jr. *Evolution of a Federalist: William Loughton Smith of Charleston*. Columbia, S.C.: University of South Carolina Press, 1962.

Rutledge, Anna Wells, ed. *The Pennsylvania Academy of Fine Arts: 1807-1870*. Philadelphia: American Philosophical Society, 1955.

Saraicks, Ambrose, *Pierre Samuel DuPont de Nemours*. Lawrence, Kans.: University of Kansas Press, 1965.

Sauvigny, Guillaume de Bertier de. "American Travelers in France, 1814-1848." In *Diplomacy in the Age of Nationalism*, edited by Nancy Barker and Marvin Brown. The Hague: Martinus Nijhoff, 1971.

Schama, Simon. *Patriots and Liberators: Revolution in the Netherlands, 1780-1813*. New York: Alfred Knopf, 1977.

Scudder, H. E., ed. *Recollections of Samuel Breck*. Philadelphia: Porter & Coates, 1877.

Seaburg, Carl and Paterson, Stanley, *Merchant Prince of Boston*. Cambridge: Harvard University Press, 1971.

Shackelford, George G. "William Short: Diplomat in Revolutionary France, 1785-1793." *American Philosophical Society Proceedings*. 102(1958): 596-612.

Shaw, Peter. *The Character of John Adams*. Chapel Hill, N.C.: University of North Carolina Press, 1976.

Shipton, Clifford, ed. *Biographical Sketches of Those Who Attended Harvard*, 17 vols. Boston: Massachusetts Historical Society, 1873-1975.

Sizer, Theodore, ed. *The Autobiography of John Trumbull*, New Haven, Conn. Yale University Press, 1953.

Smelser, Marshall. *The Congress Founds the Navy, 1787-1798*. South Bend, Ind.: University of Notre Dame Press, 1959.

————. "The Federalist Period as an Age of Passion." *American Quarterly* 10(1958): 391-419.

Smith, Joseph E. A. *The History of Pittsfield*. Boston, Mass.: Lee & Shepard, 1876.

Smith, James M., *Freedom's Fetters*. Ithaca, N.Y.: Cornell University Press, 1966.

Smith, Page. *John Adams*, 2 vols. New York: Doubleday & Company, 1962.

Snow, Vernon F., ed. "The Grand Tour Diary of Robert C. Johnson, 1792-1793." *American Philosophical Society Proceedings* 102 (1958): 60-104.

Steiner, Bernard, *Life and Correspondence of James McHenry*. Cleveland, Ohio: Burrow Brothers & Company, 1907.

Stern, Jean. *Belle et Bonne*. Paris: Hachette, 1938.

Stewart, Donald H. *The Opposition Press of the Federalist Period*. Albany: State University of New York Press, 1969.

Stinchcombe, William. *The American Revolution and the French Alliance*. Syracuse, N.Y.: Syracuse University Press, 1969.

————. "A Neglected Memoir by Talleyrand on French-American Relations." *American Philosophical Society Proceedings* 121 (1977): 195-208.

————. "L'alliance franco-américaine après l'Indépendance." In *Le Règne de Louis XVI et la Guerre d'Indépendance américaine*, edited by Jean de Vigeurie. Dourgne, France, 1979. 121-40.

————. "Talleyrand and The American Negotiations of 1797-1798." *Journal of American History* 62 (1975): 575-90.

————. "The Diplomacy of the WXYZ Affair." *William and Mary Quarterly* 34 (1977): 590-617.

Stoddard, T. Lothrop. *The French Revolution in Santo Domingo.* Westport, Conn.: Negro Universities Press, 1970.

Swan, Michel M. *The Athenaeum Gallery.* Boston: Boston Athenaeum, 1940.

Szramkiewicz, Romauld. *Les Régents et Censeurs de la Banque nommes sous le Consultat et l'Empire.* Geneva: E. Droz, 1974.

Thompson, Mack. "Causes and Circumstances of the DuPont Family's Emigration." *French Historical Studies* 6 (1969): 59-77.

Trescott, William H. *The Diplomatic History of the Administrations of Washington and Adams.* Boston: Little, Brown & Company, 1857.

Turner, Frederick J. "The Policy of France Toward the Mississippi Valley in the Period of Washington and Adams." *American Historical Review* 10 (1905): 249-79.

Turner, Orestus. *History of the Pioneer Settlement of Phelps and Gormans Purchase and Morris Reserve.* Rochester, N.Y.: W. Ailing, 1851.

Watson, F. J. B., *The Wrightman Collection,* 2 vols. Greenwich, Conn.: New York Graphic Society, 1966.

Wehtje, Myron F. "The Congressional Elections of 1799 in Virginia." *West Virginia History* 24 (1968) 251-58.

Weiner, Margery. *The French Exiles: 1789-1815.* New York: William Morrow & Company, 1961.

Welch, Richard E., Jr. *Theodore Sedgwick, Federalist: A Political Portrait.* Middletown, Conn.: Wesleyan University Press, 1965.

Winter, Pieter J. van *Het Aandeel van de Amsterdamschen handel aan den opbouw van het Amerikaansche Gemeenebest,* 2 vols. The Hague: Martinus Nijhoff, 1927, 1933.

Woloch, Isser. *Jacobin Legacy.* Princeton, N.J.: Princeton University Press, 1970.

Woodress, James. *A Yankee's Odyssey: The Life of Joel Barlow.* Philadelphia: Lippincott & Company, 1958.

Yorke, Henry R. *Letters from France,* 2 vols. London: Sherwood, 1814.

Zahniser, Marvin. *Charles Cotesworth Pinckney.* Chapel Hill, N.C.: University of North Carolina Press, 1967.

Dissertations

Averill, Louise. "John Vanderlyn, American Painter." Ph.D. Dissertation, Yale University, 1949.

Babb, Winston, C. "French Refugees from Saint Domingue to the Southern United States." Ph.D. Dissertation, University of Virginia, 1954.

Baldridge, Edwin R. "Talleyrand in the United States, 1794-1796." Ph.D. Dissertation, Lehigh University, 1963.

Davis, William A. "William Constable: New York Merchant and Land Speculator, 1772-1803." Ph.D. Dissertation, Harvard University, 1956.

Gard, René Coulet du, "Les Francais exilés, émigrés, réfugiés en Pennsylvania de 1789 à 1800." Ph.D. Dissertation, Université de Besançon, 1966.

Homan, Gerlof. "The Revolutionary Career of Jean Francois Reubell." Ph.D. Dissertation, University of Kansas, 1958.

Hugill, Peter J. "A Small Town Landscape as a Sustained Gesture on the Part of a Dominant Social Group: Cazenovia, New York, 1794-1976." Ph.D. Dissertation, Syracuse University, 1977.

Keuhl, Joel W. "Quest for Identity: The XYZ Affair and American Nationalism." Ph.D. Dissertation, University of Wisconsin, 1968.

Merz, Nancy M. "The XYZ Affair and the Congressional Election of 1799 in Richmond, Virginia." M.A. thesis, College of Wiliam and Mary, 1973.

O'Dwyer, Margaret. "Louis Guillaume Otto in America." Ph.D. Dissertation, Northwestern University, 1954.

Ramusson, Ethel E. "Capital on the Delaware: The Philadelphia Upper Class in Transition, 1789-1801." Ph.D. Dissertation, Brown University, 1962.

Shackelford, George G. "William Short: Jefferson's Adopted Son, 1758-1849." Ph.D. Dissertation, University of Virginia, 1955.

Smith, Ronald D., "French Interests in Louisiana from Choiseul to Napoleon." Ph.D. Dissertation, University of Southern California, 1964.

Index

Adams, John, 6, 10, 11, 27, 53, 111, 112, 117, 119; accepts Hamilton's ideas, 23; address to Congress, 20-21; appoints envoys, 18, 21; attitude toward French Revolution, 14-15; backs Gerry, 113; between parties, 15; break with Vergennes, 16; cabinet meeting, 20; calls special session of Congress, 19; changes French policy, 120-21; conflicts with Federalists, 11; criticism of, 119-20; defeat in 1800, 129; denounces France, 118; failure with Republicans, 15; French demand apology for his speech, 3, 41, 42; French view of him, 39; influence of American Revolution on, 25; list of possible appointments, 22, 30; offers post to Madison, 13; opinion of Franklin, 16; policy toward France, 16-17; political strength of, 17; relations with cabinet, 17; relations with Senate, 22; replies of cabinet members, 20; requests advice of cabinet, 19; talks with Jefferson, 13; view of Monroe, 24; view of XYZ affair, 125; as viewed by Americans in Paris, 97-98

Adams, John Q., 120, 126; in The Hague, 52; quoted, 35

Adams, Thomas B., in Paris, 52, 88

Adet, Pierre: advice on U.S. policy, 36; and campaign of 1796, 14, 39; French minister to the U.S., 9; opposes Jay Treaty, 9; view of Adams, 15; withdraws, 14

American envoys: Adams' speech and, 42, 55; and Bellamy, 57, 58; instructions, 15; lodging in Paris, 54; meets with Hottinguer, 57, 58; meets with Talleyrand, 54, 110-11; notice of U.S. ships captured, 85; outline of U.S. position, 108; view of French in U.S., 40. See Gerry, Elbridge; Marshall, John; Pinckney, Charles C.

Americans in Paris, 77-99; list of, 135-39; in negotiations, 110

American State Papers, reprint XYZ dispatches, 4

Andrews, Samuel, 85

Appleton, Nathaniel, 81-82

Araujo de Azevedo, Antonio de, jailed, 106

Arbelles, André d', 71

Aurora, 18, 117; on negotiations, 109; press ruined, 119

Autremont, Louis Paul d', 42; confers with Gerry, 107, 110; in negotiations, 58; secretary to Talleyrand, 35; sells land, 85

About the Author

WILLIAM STINCHCOMBE is Professor of History at Syracuse University in Syracuse, New York. His earlier books include *The American Revolution and the French Alliance* and volume III of the *Papers of John Marshall*, which he edited.